Neo Patterns Collection

Vol.01
Patientia Patterns
Coloring Book for Adults

by Asma Zergui

ISBN-13:
978-1508958949

ISBN-10:
1508958947

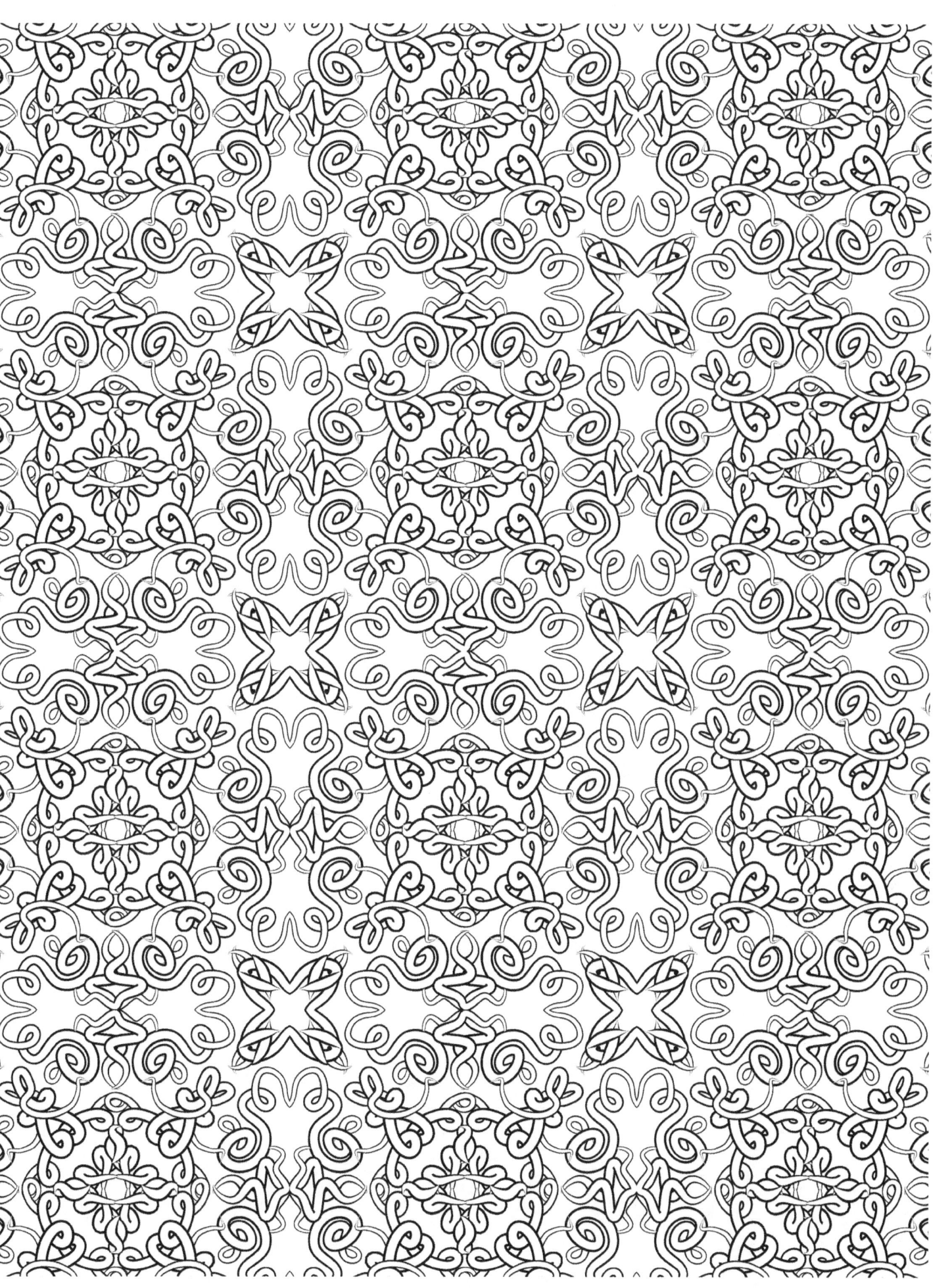

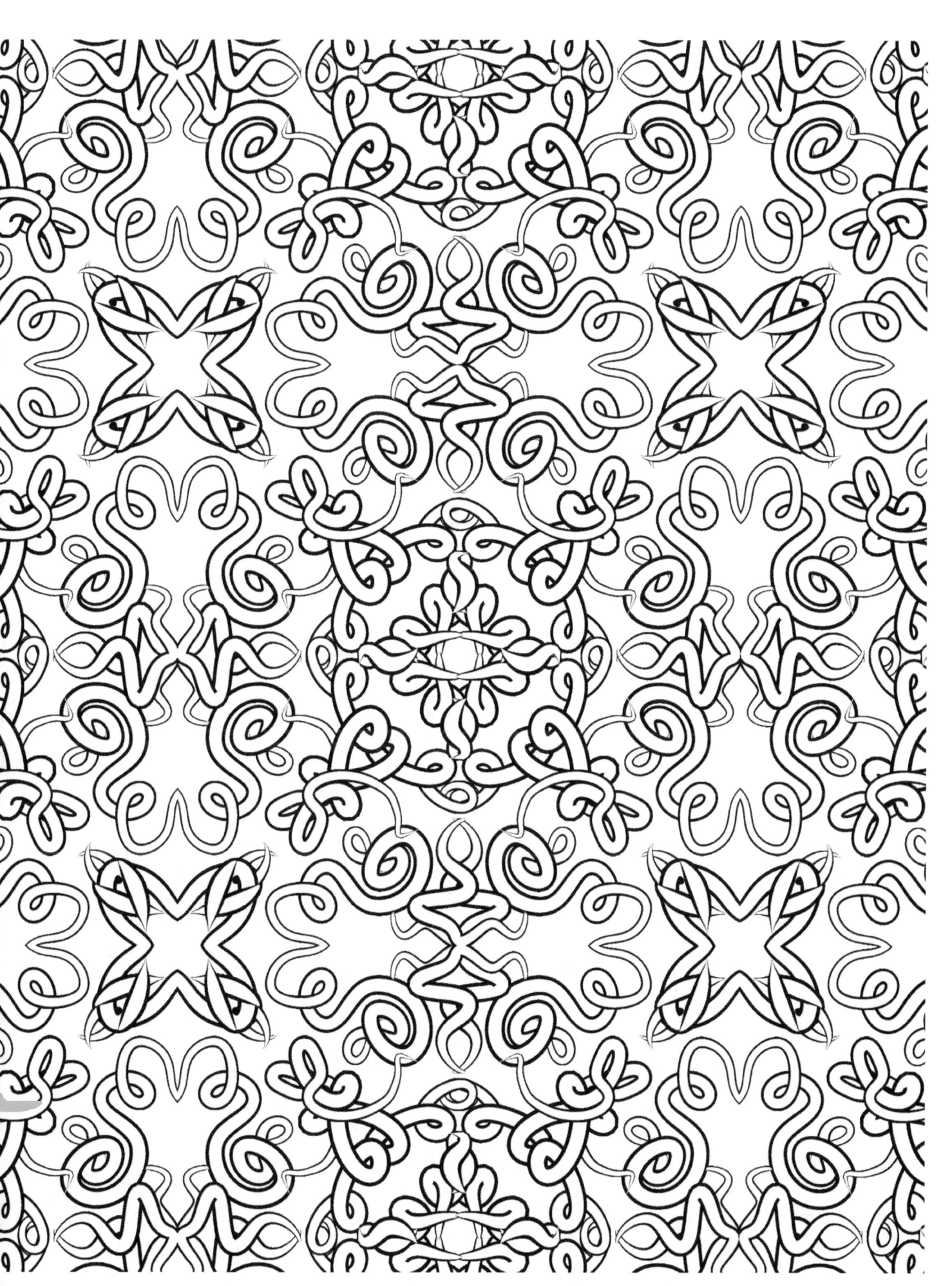

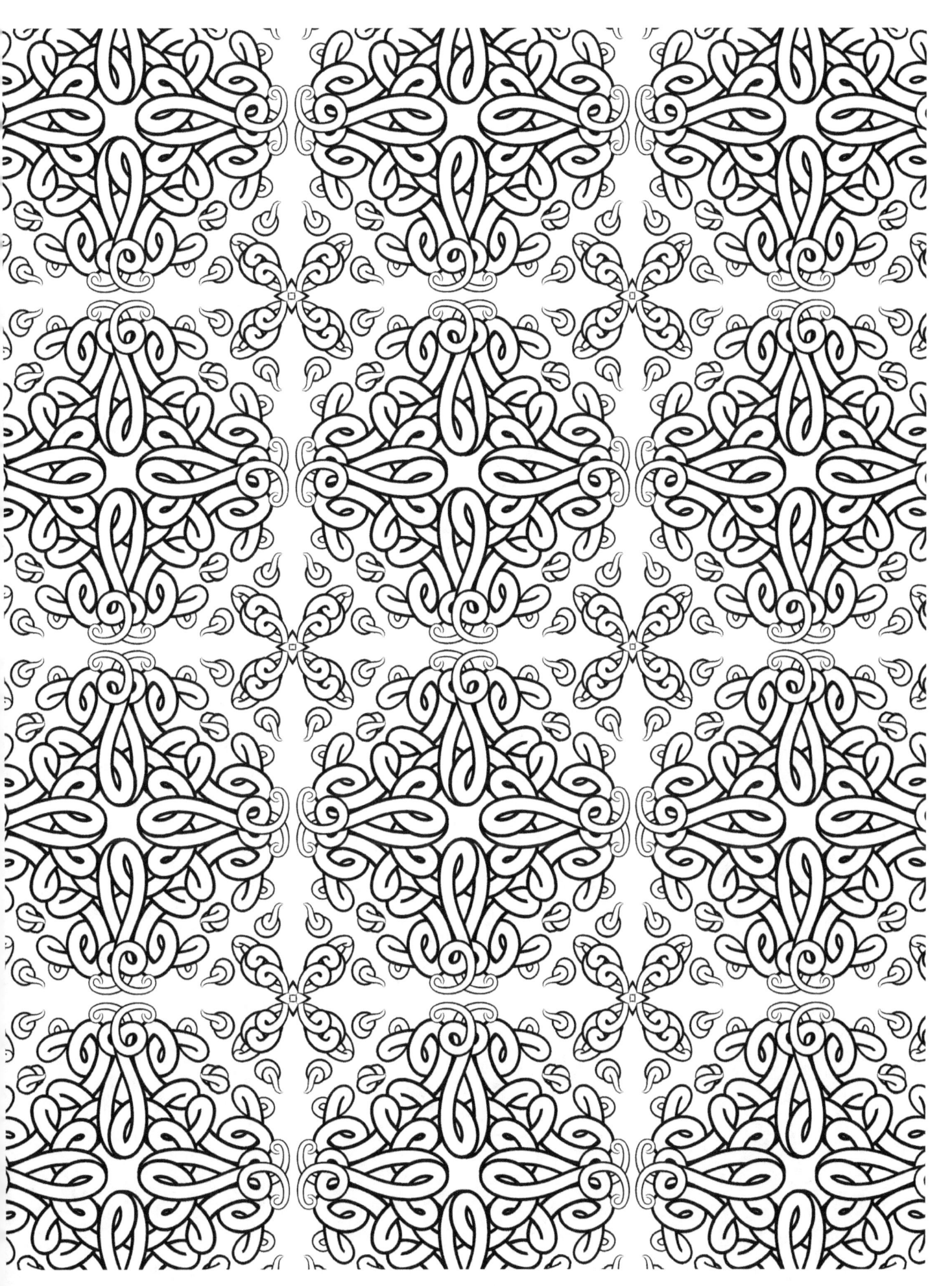

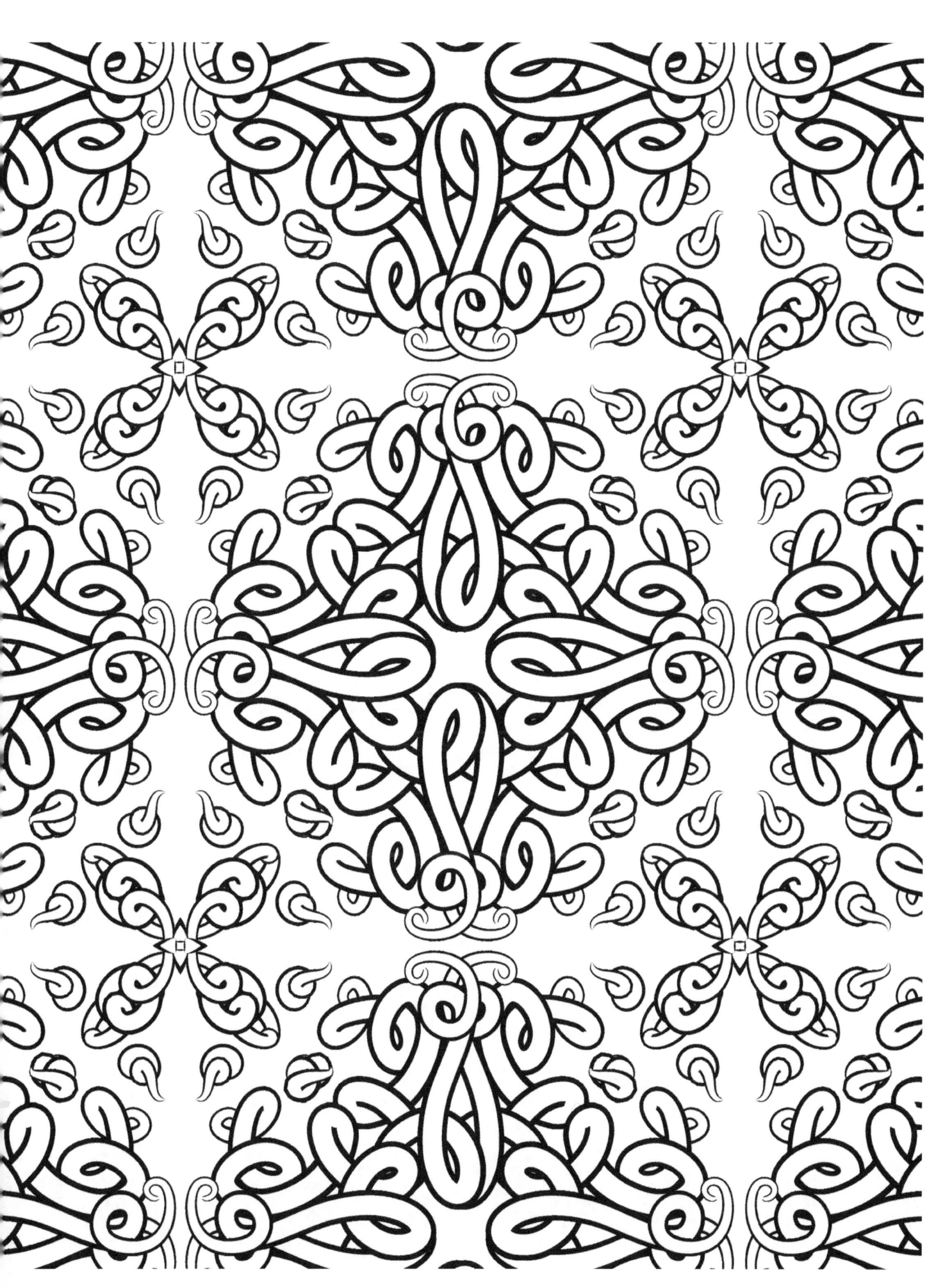

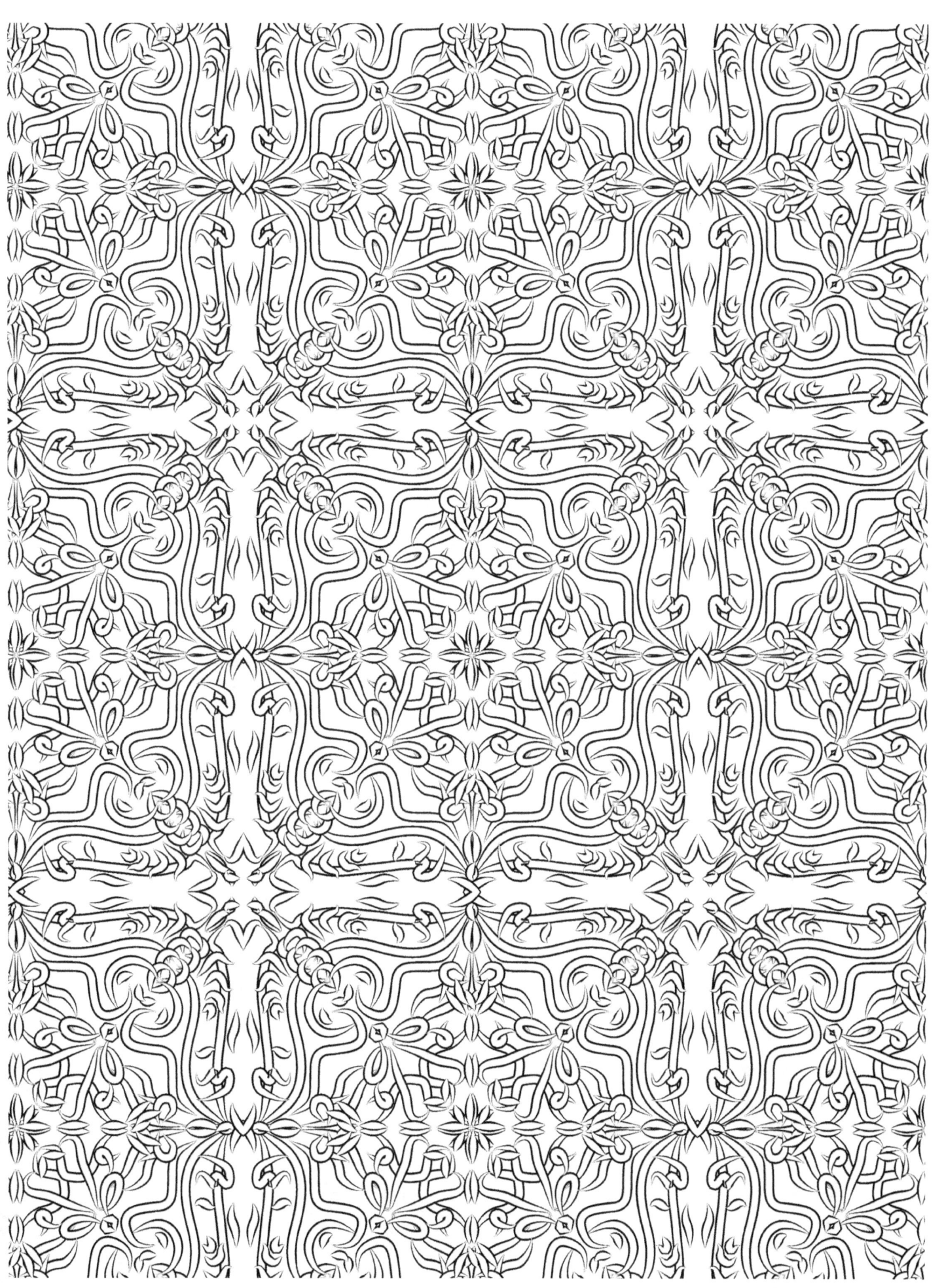

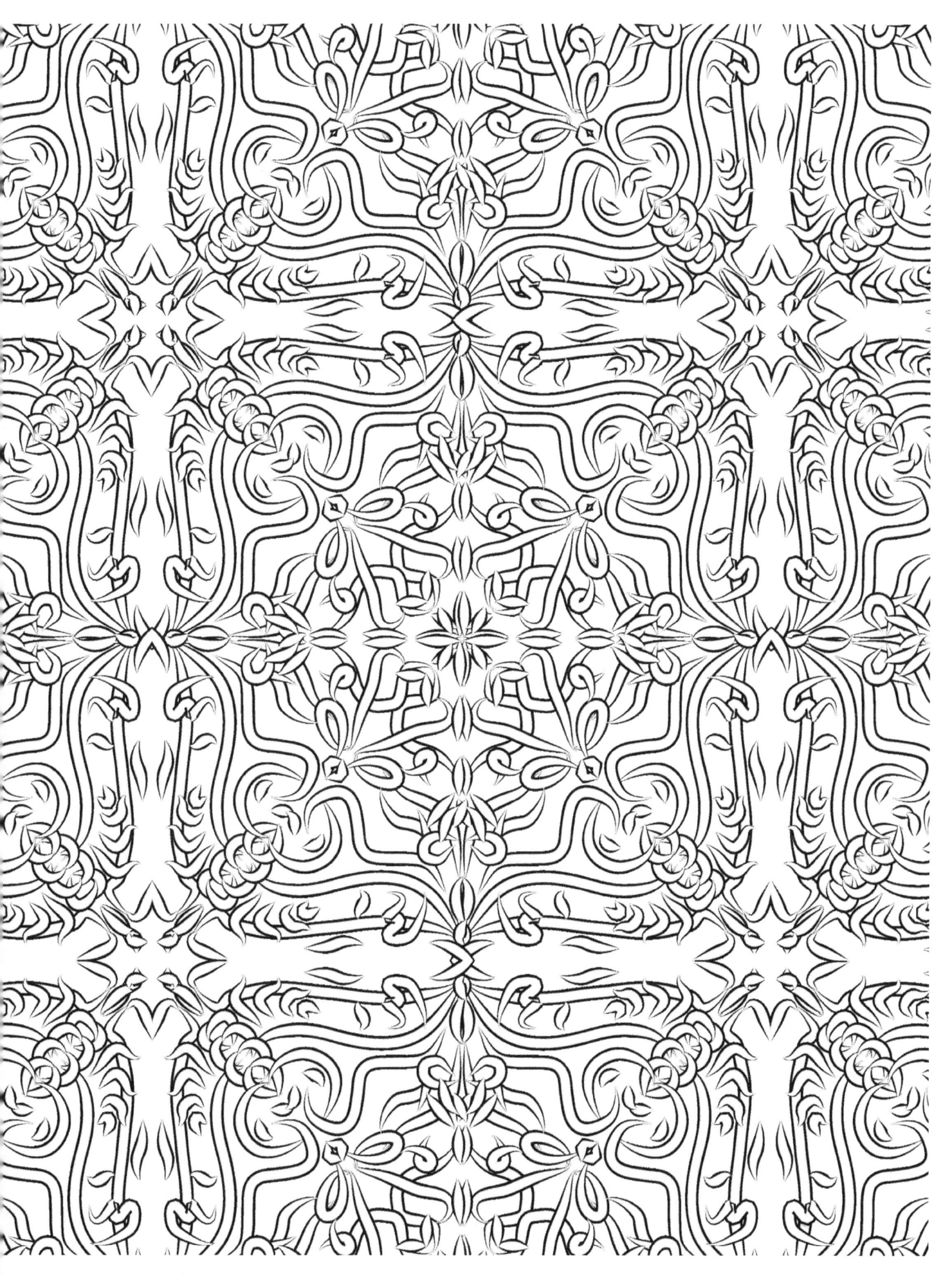

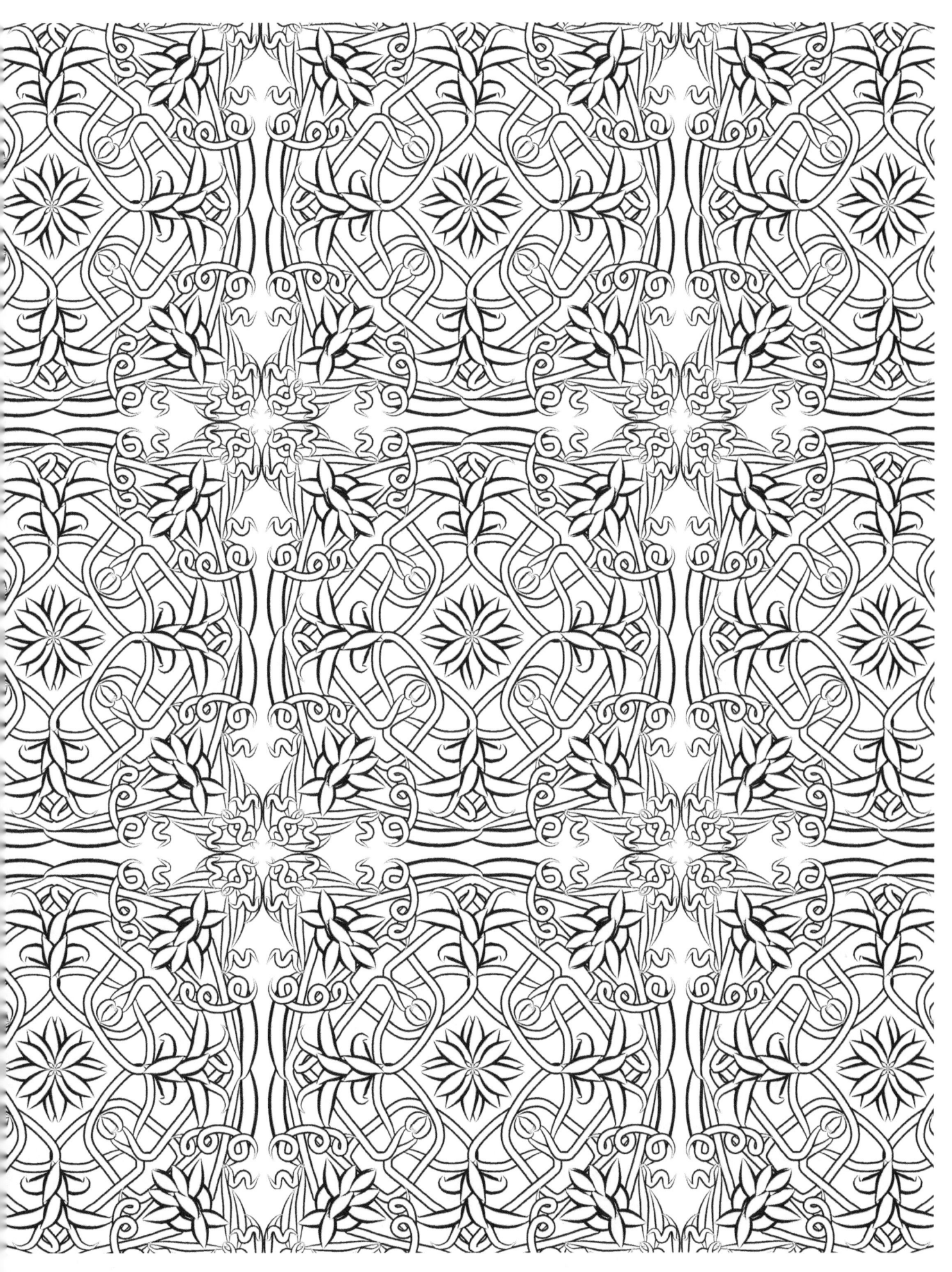

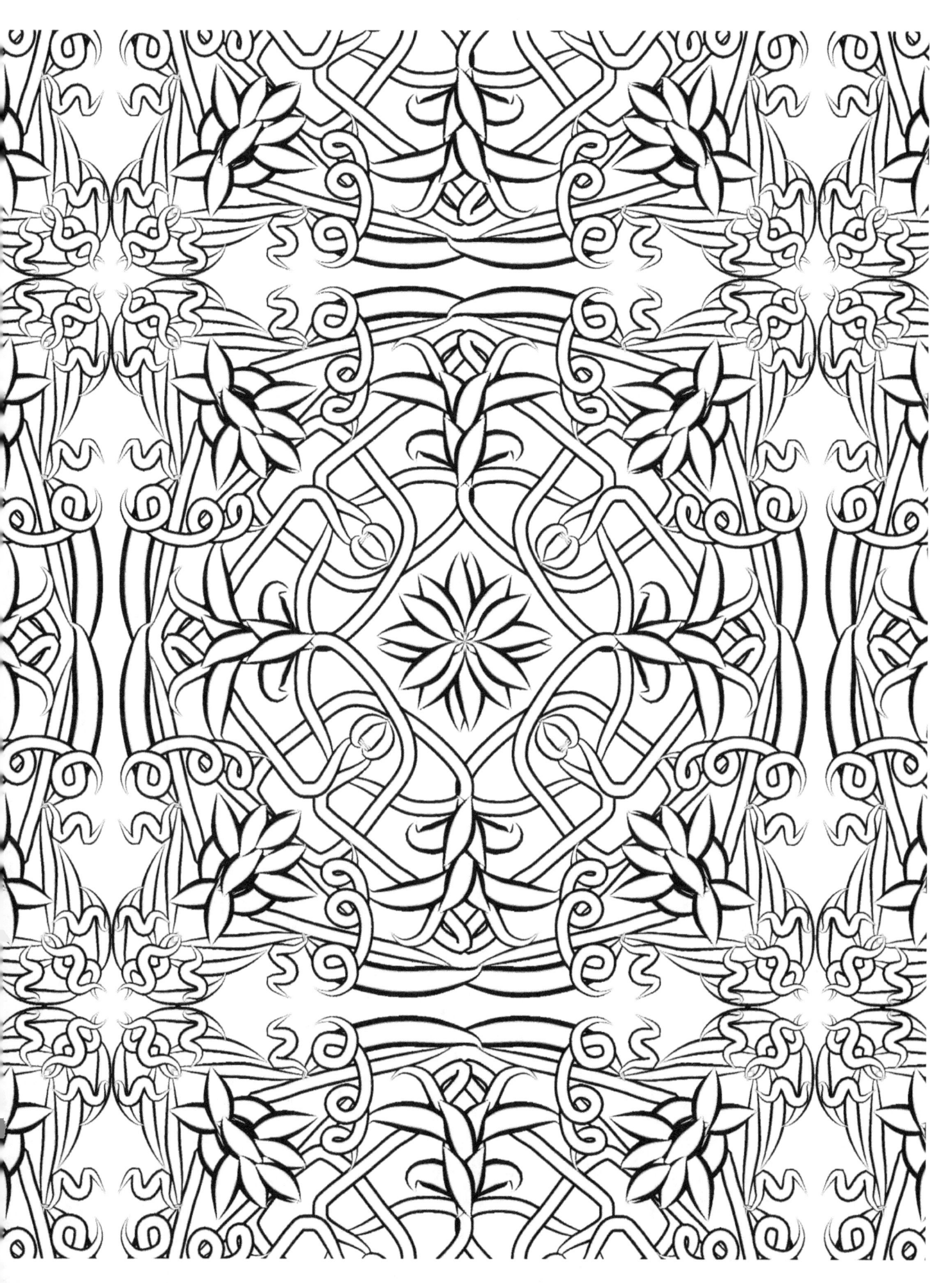

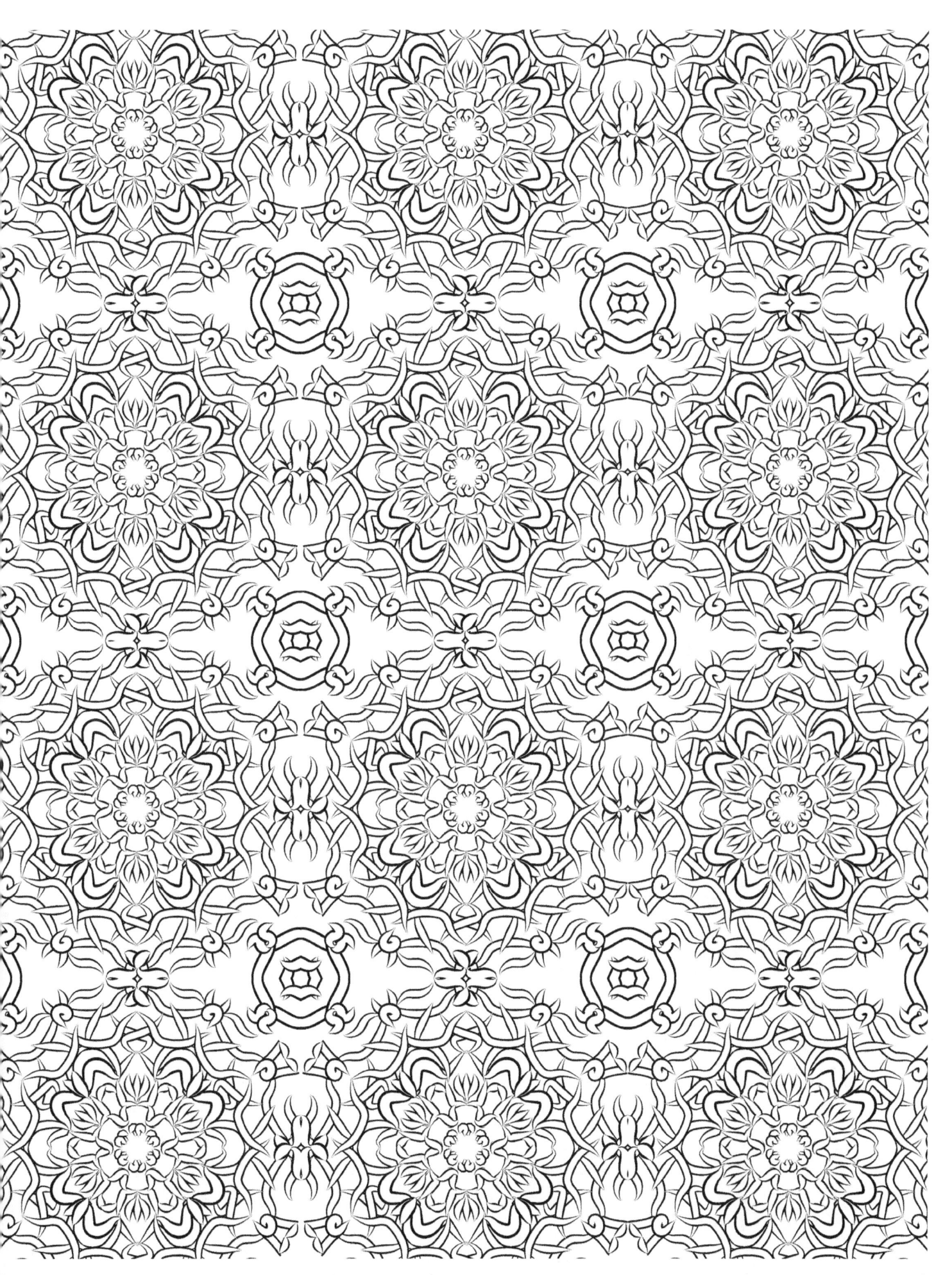

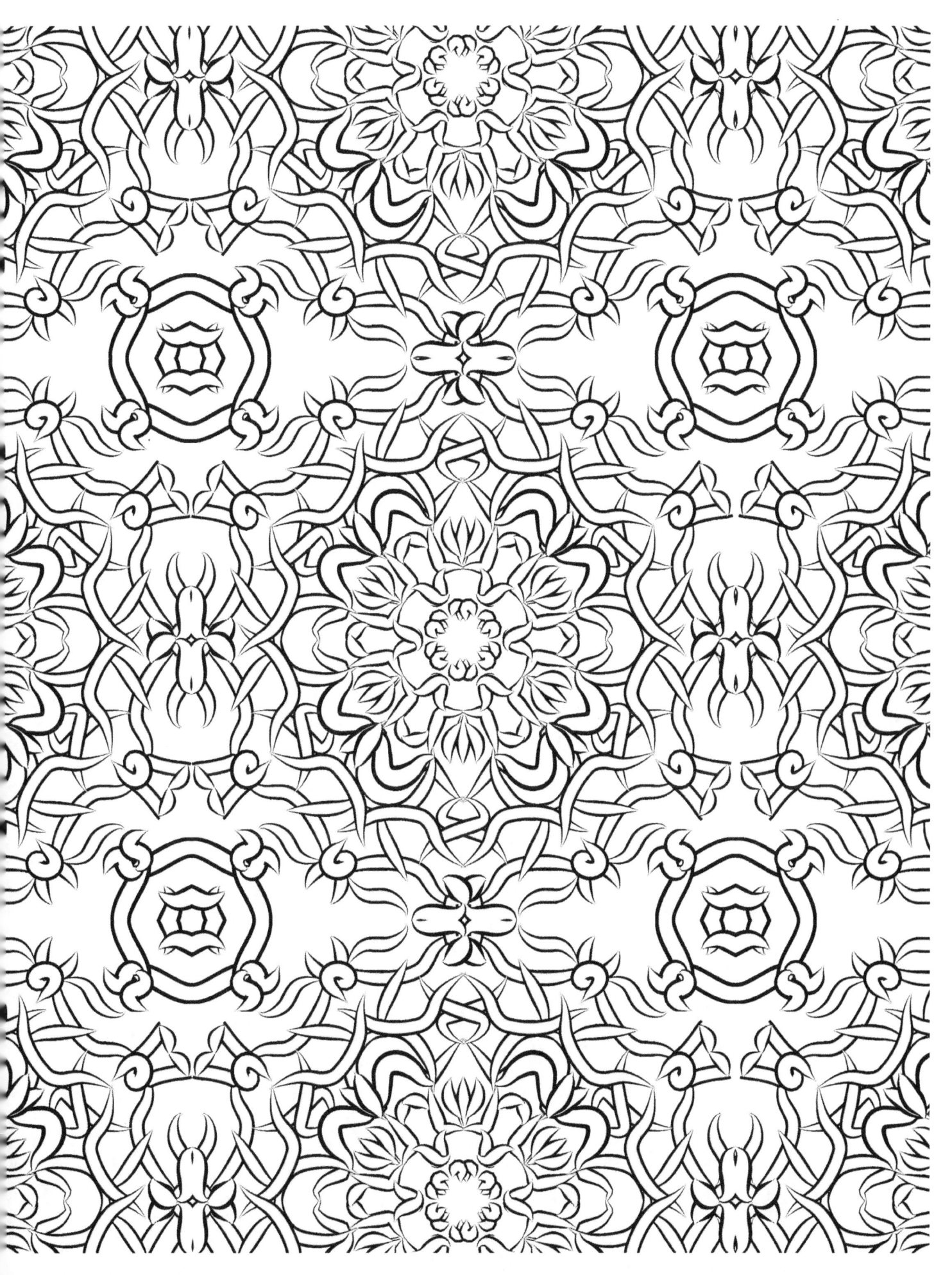

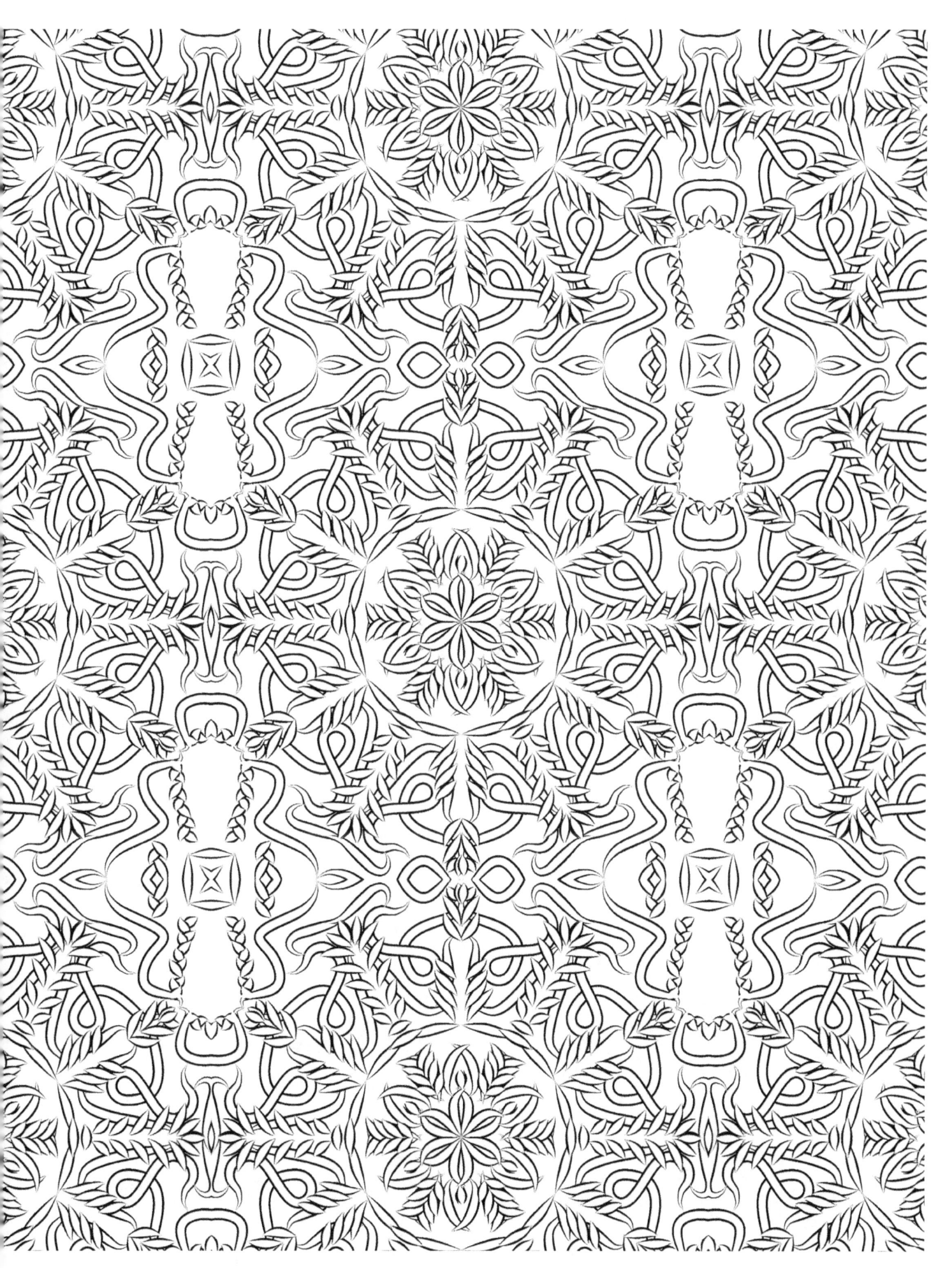

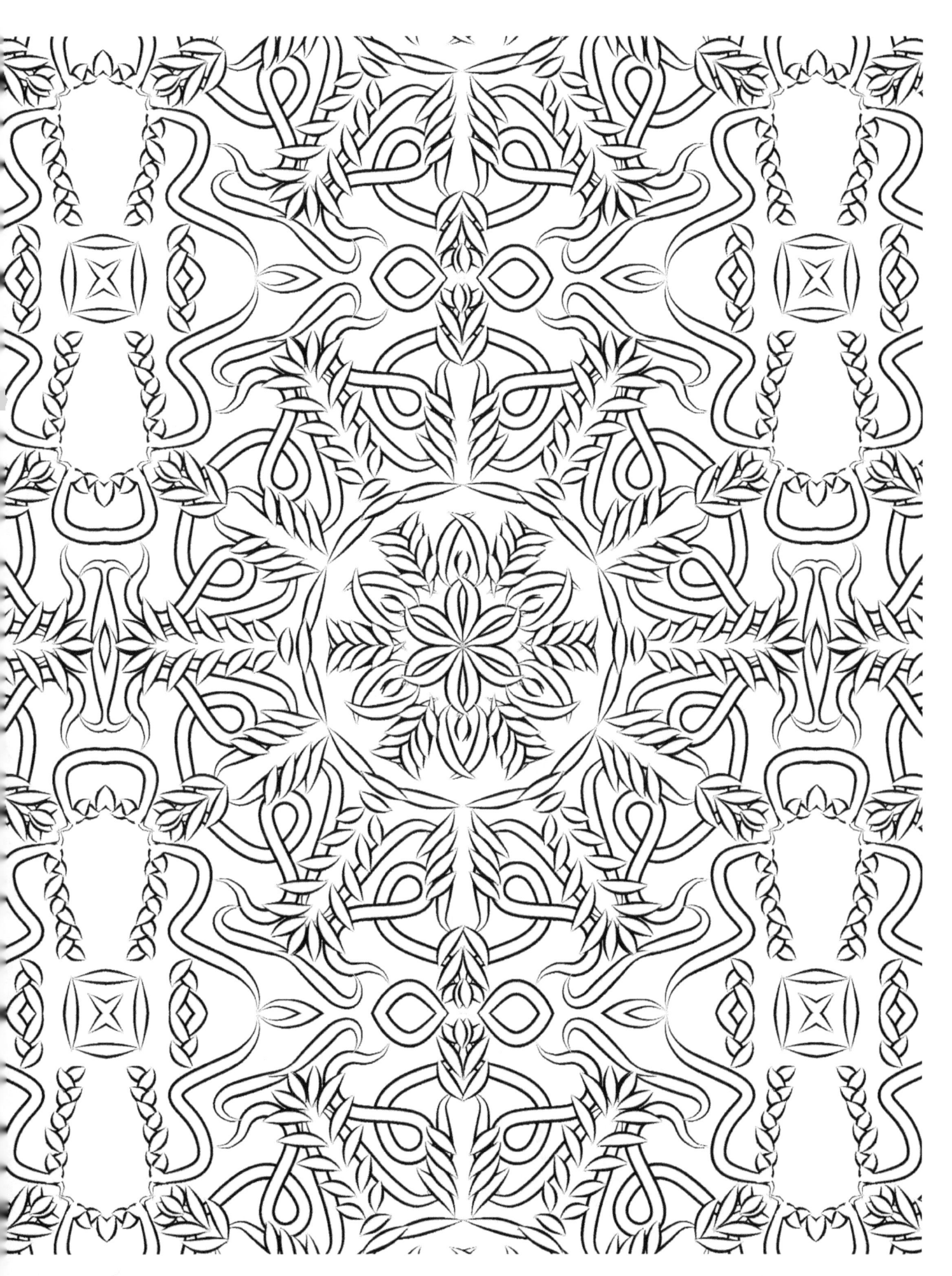

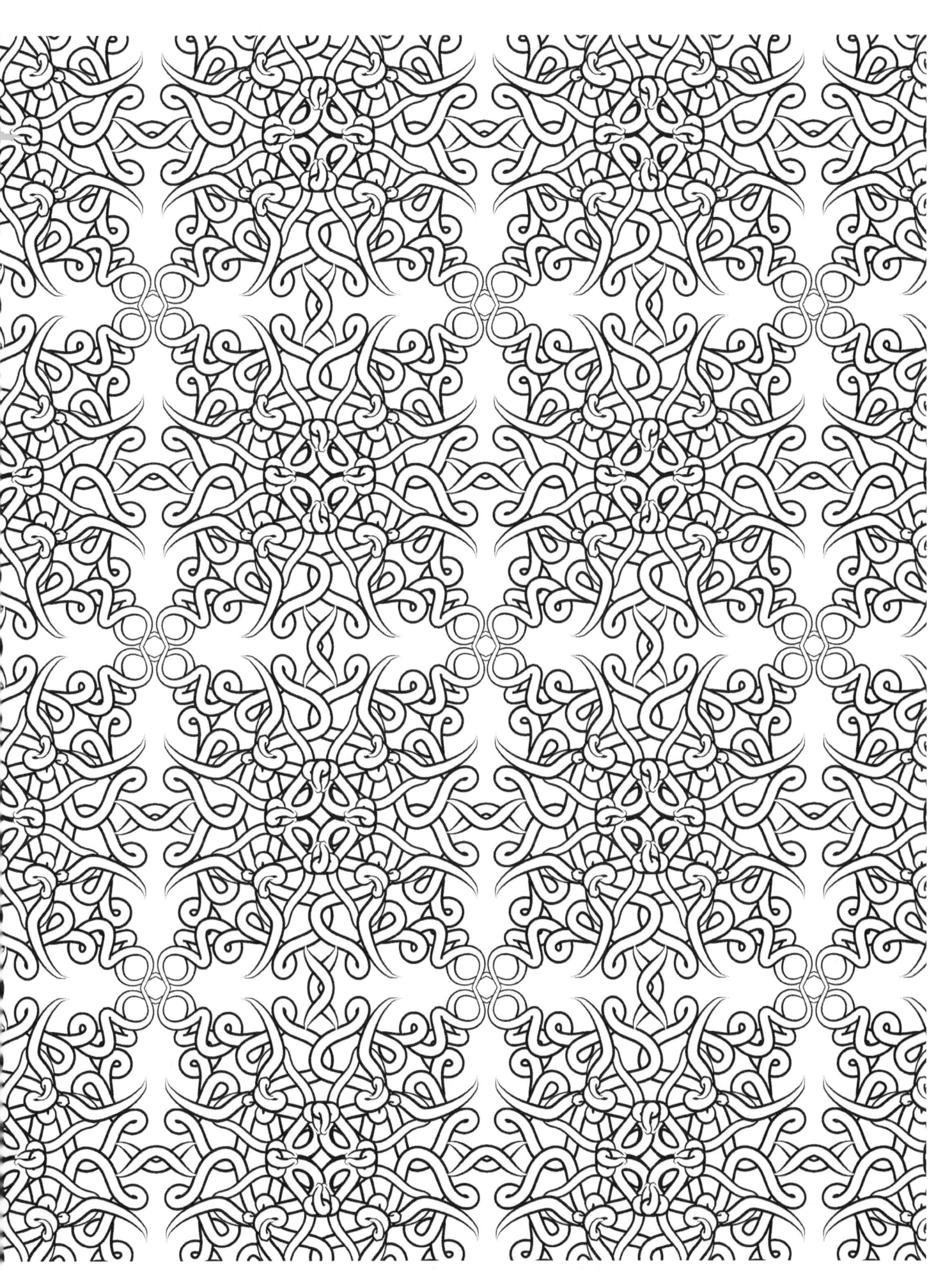

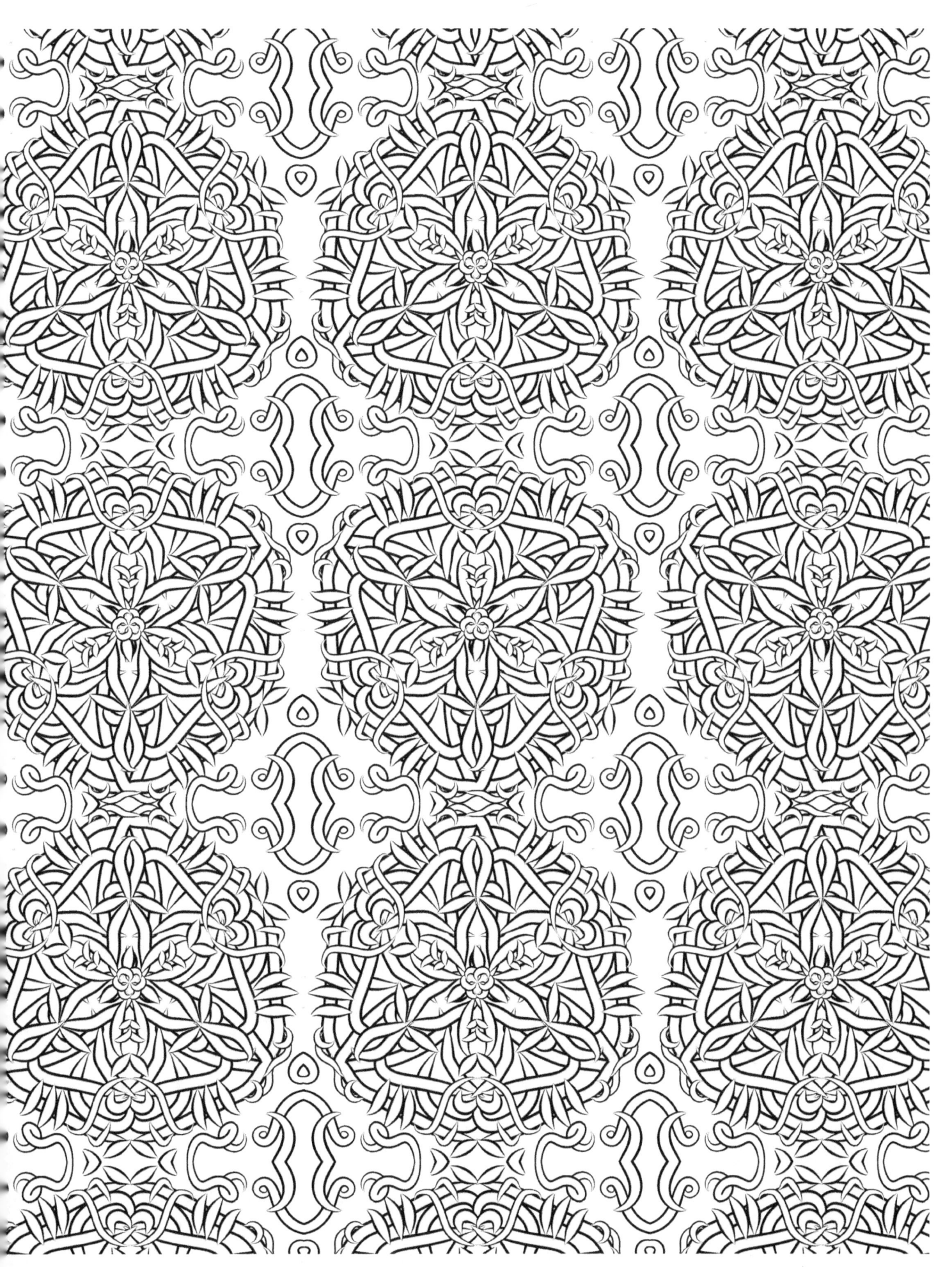

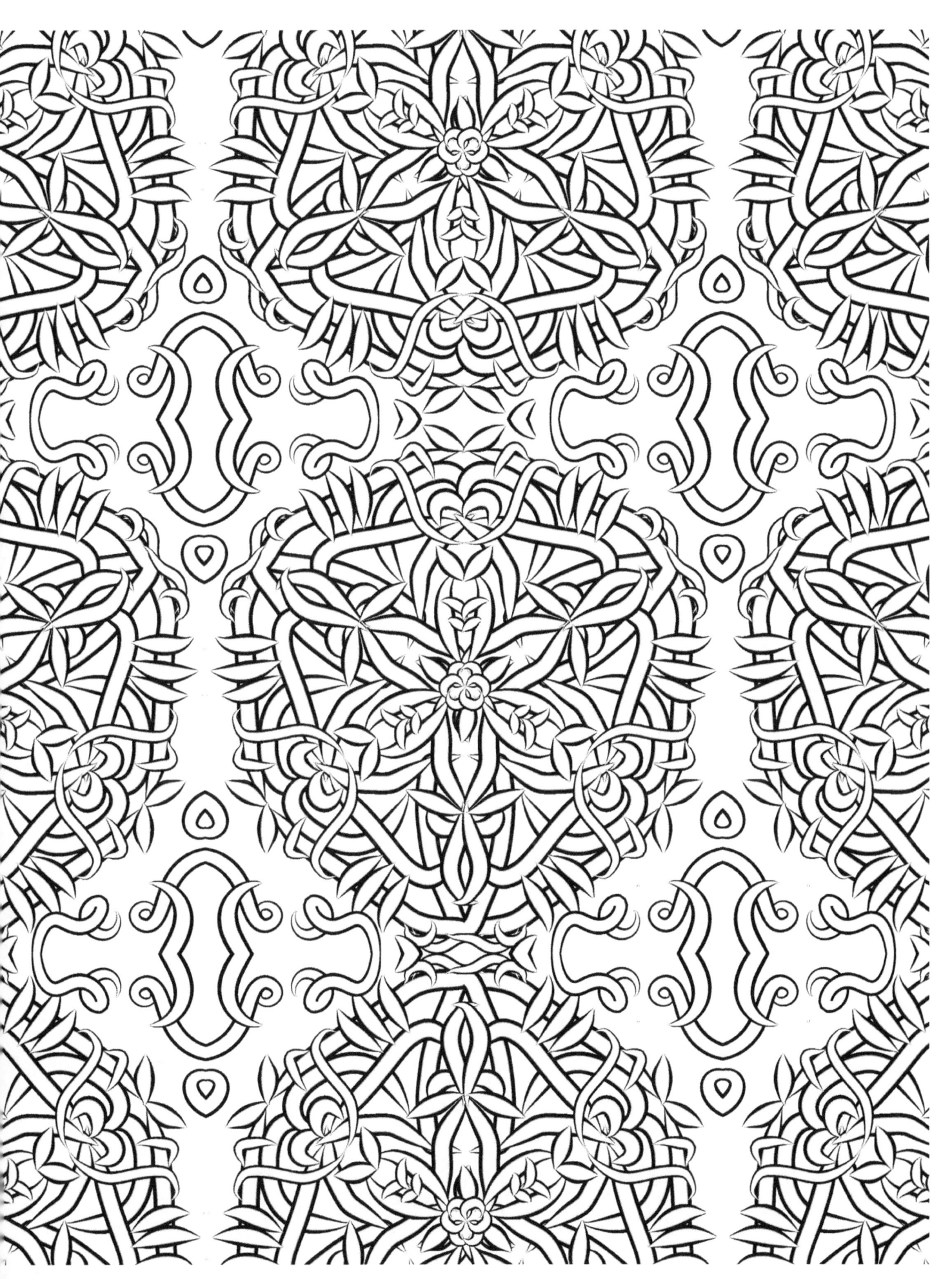

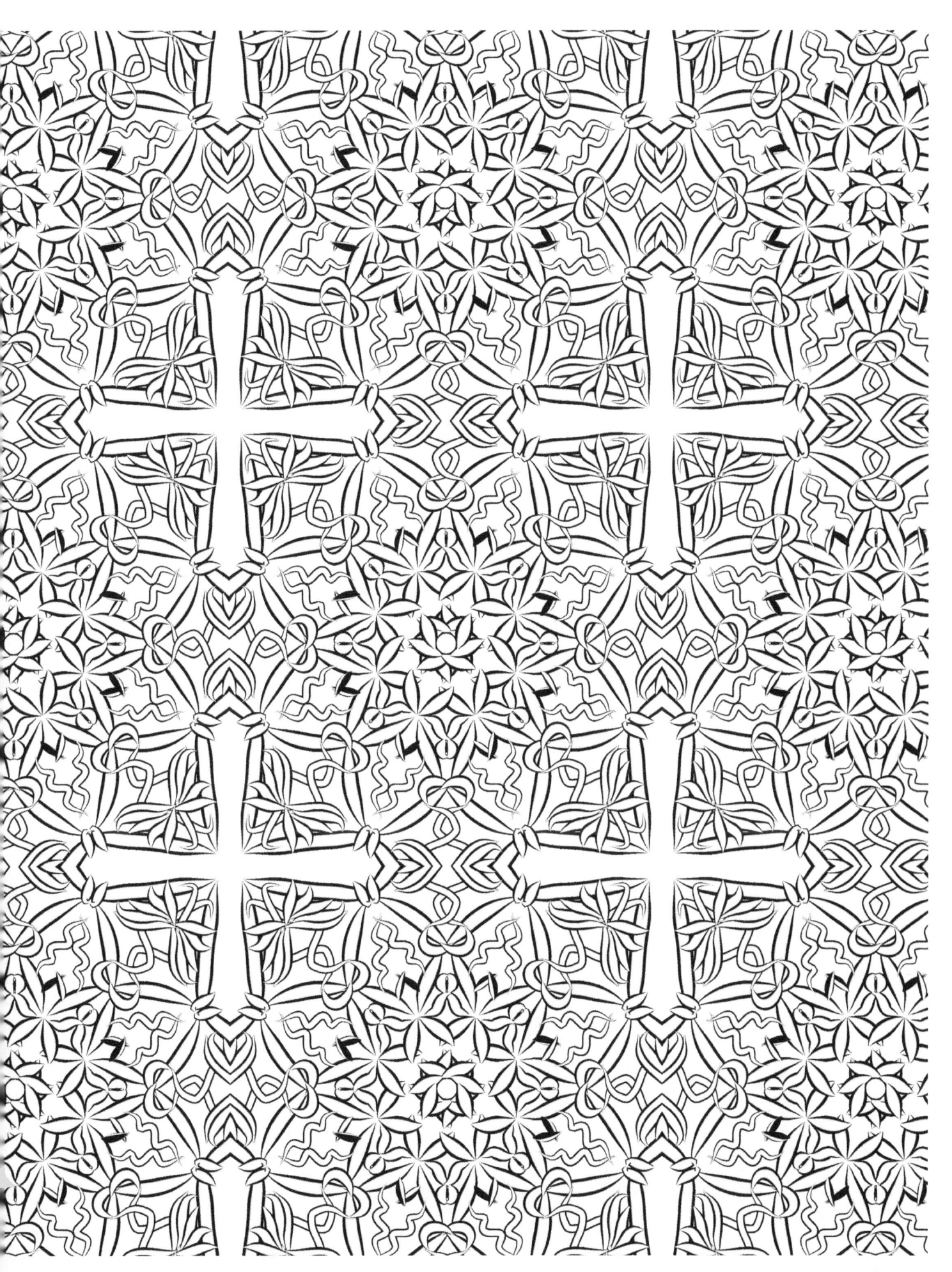

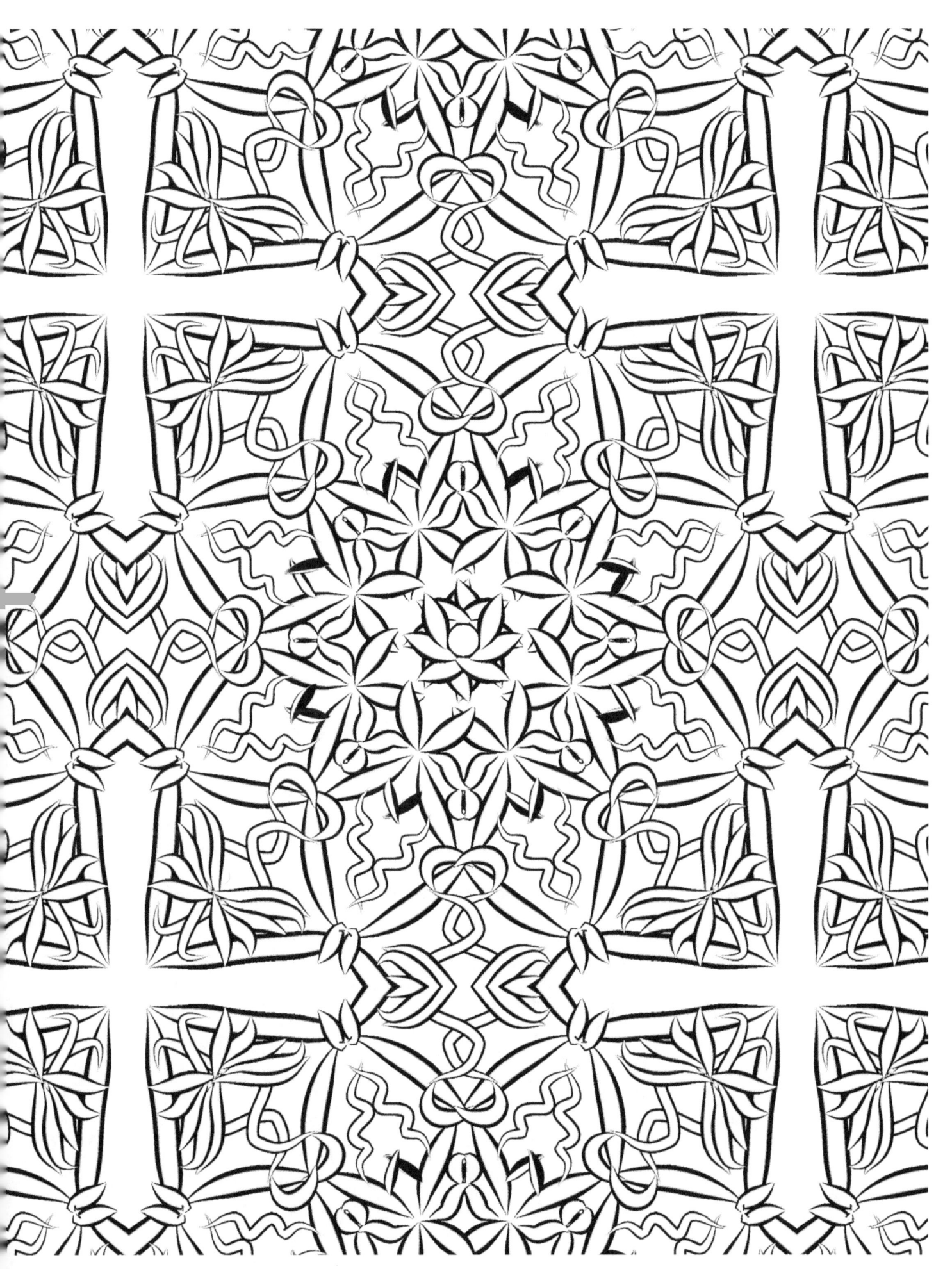

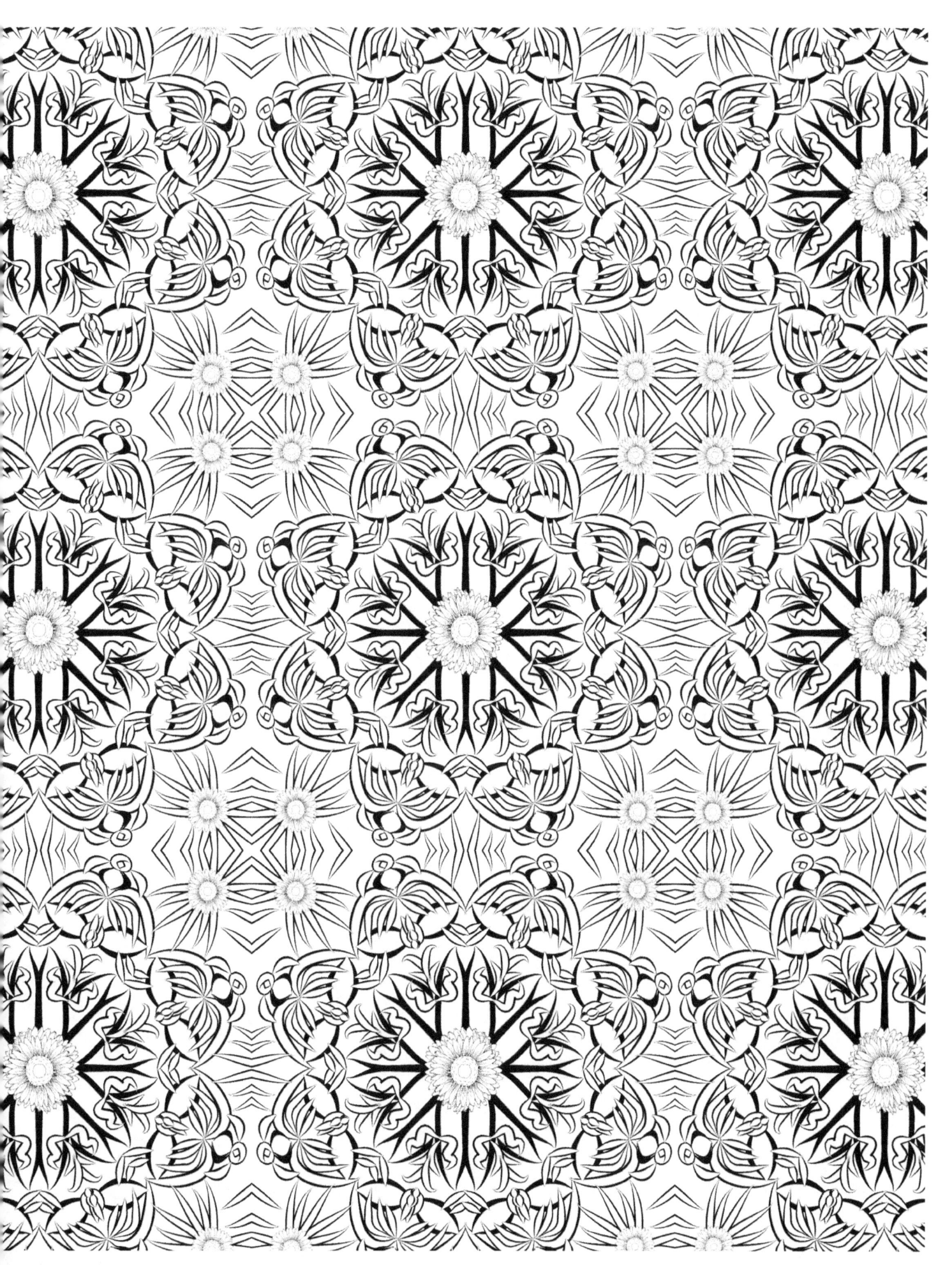

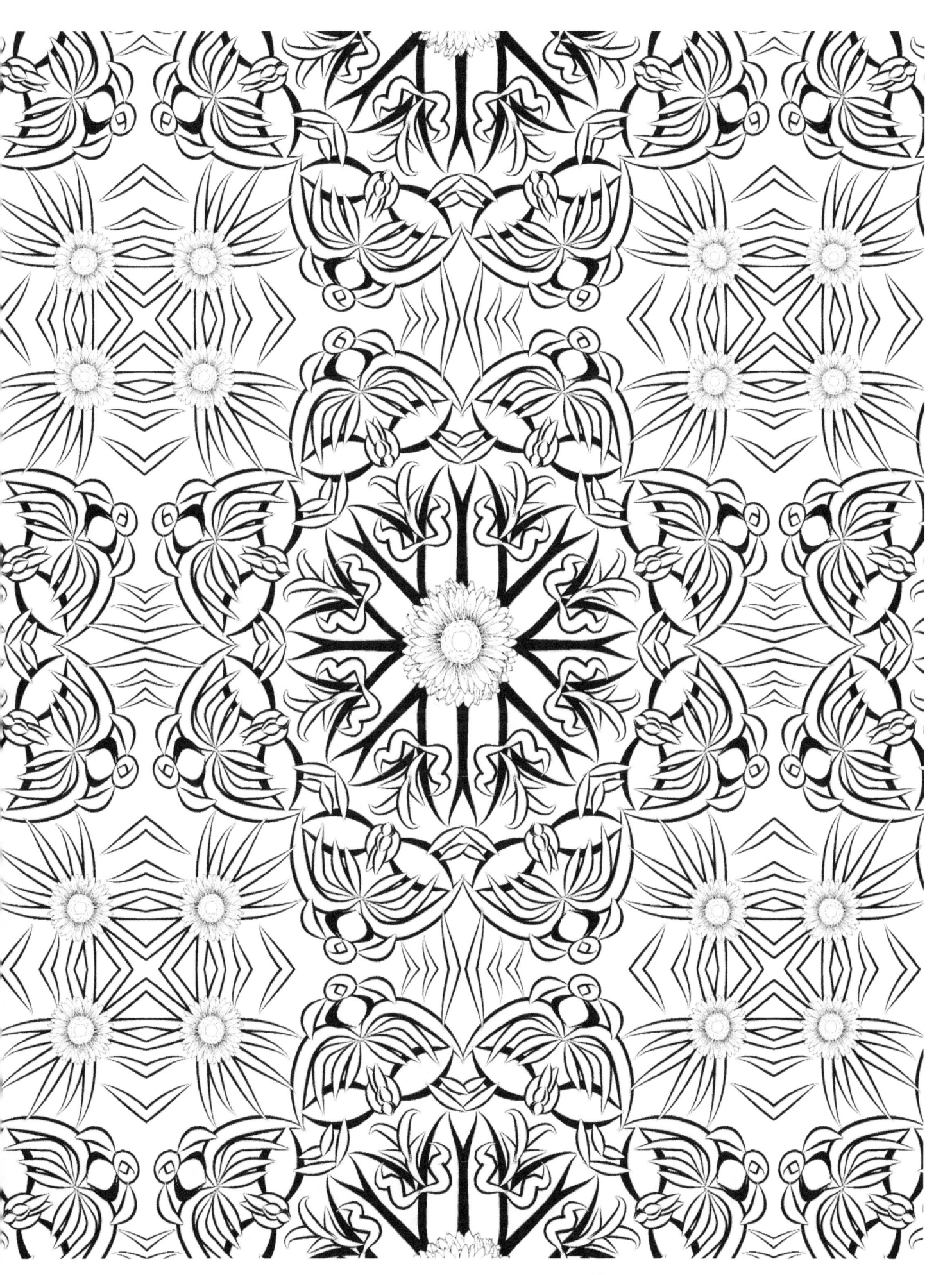

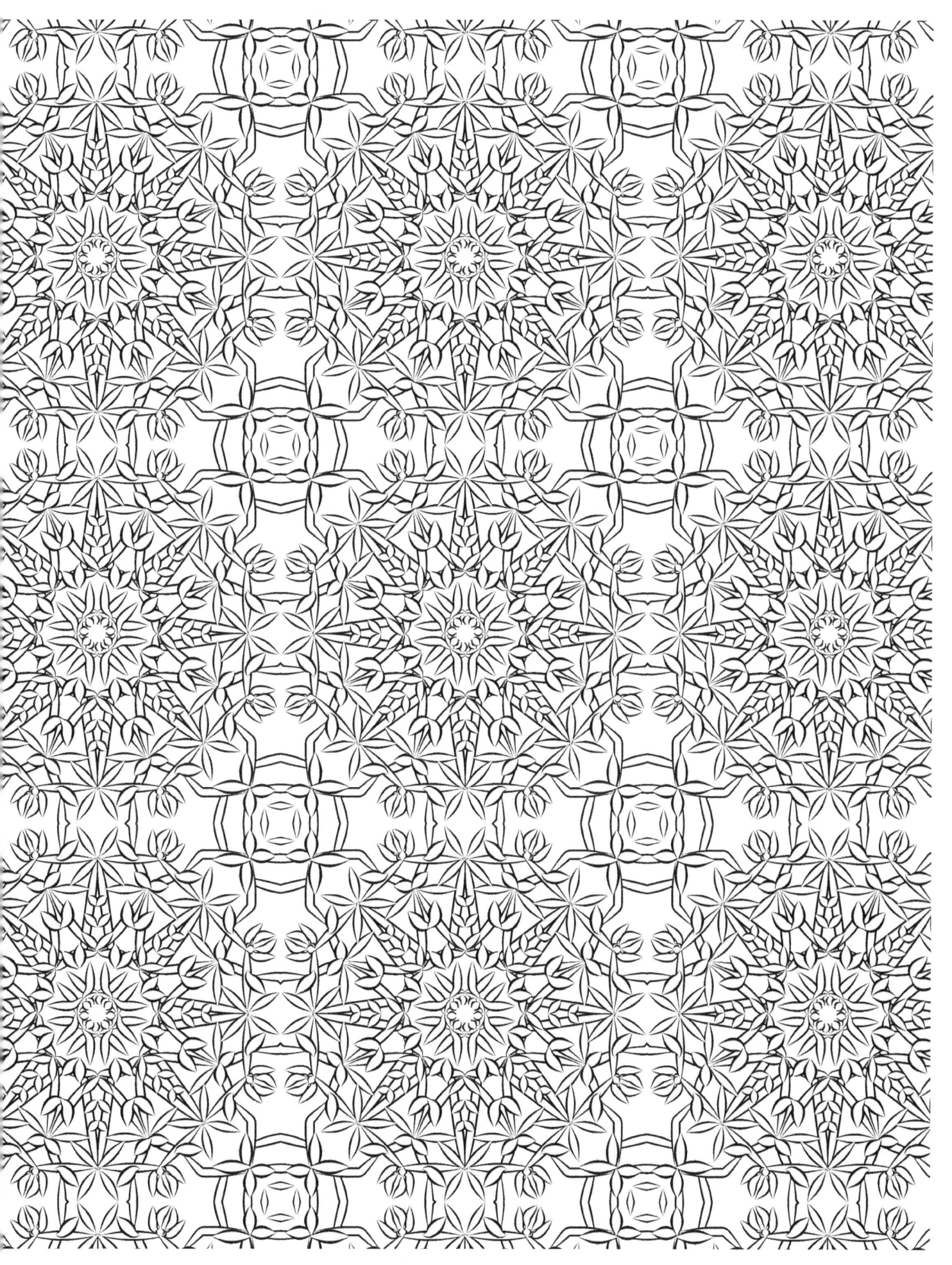

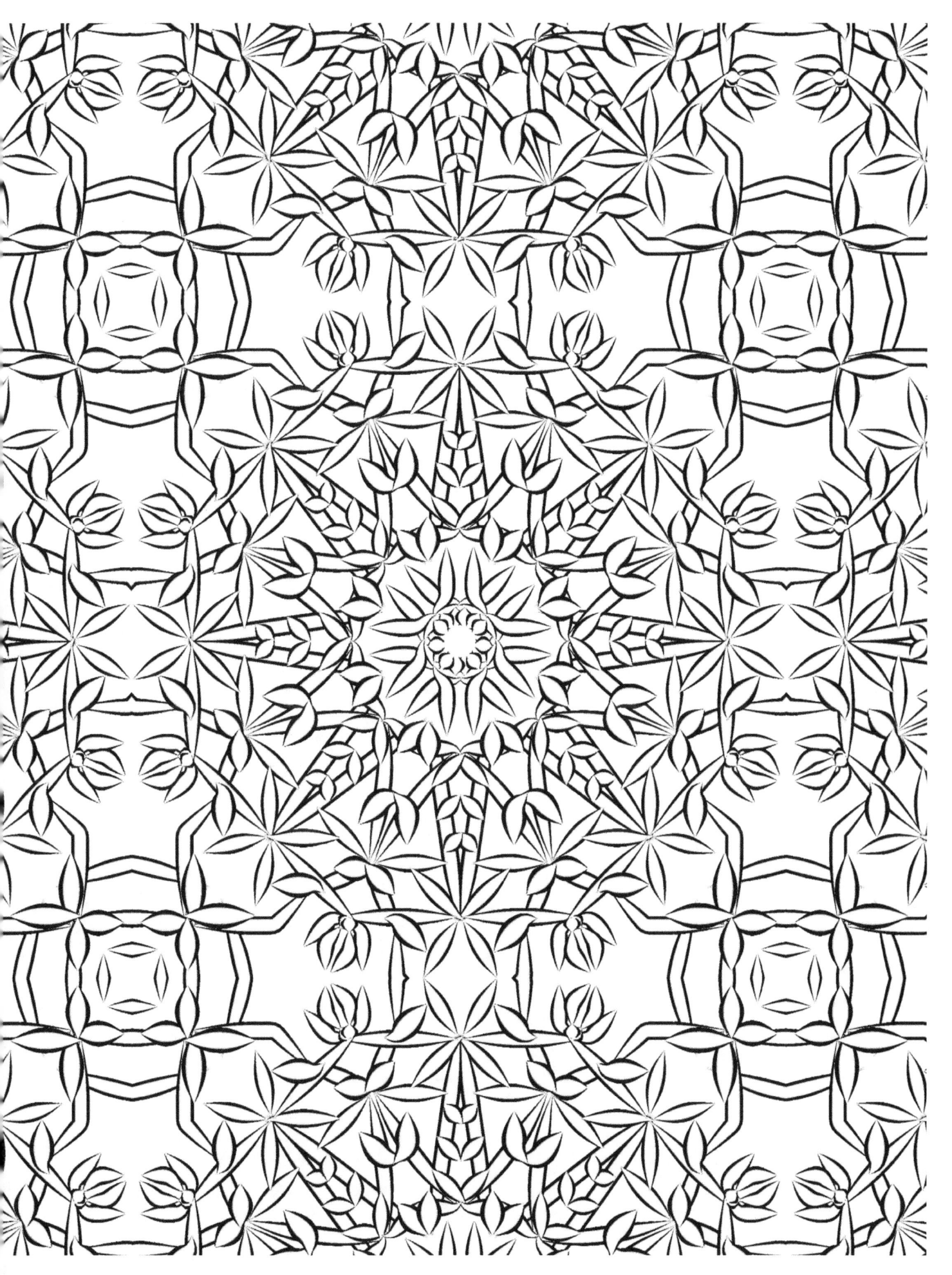

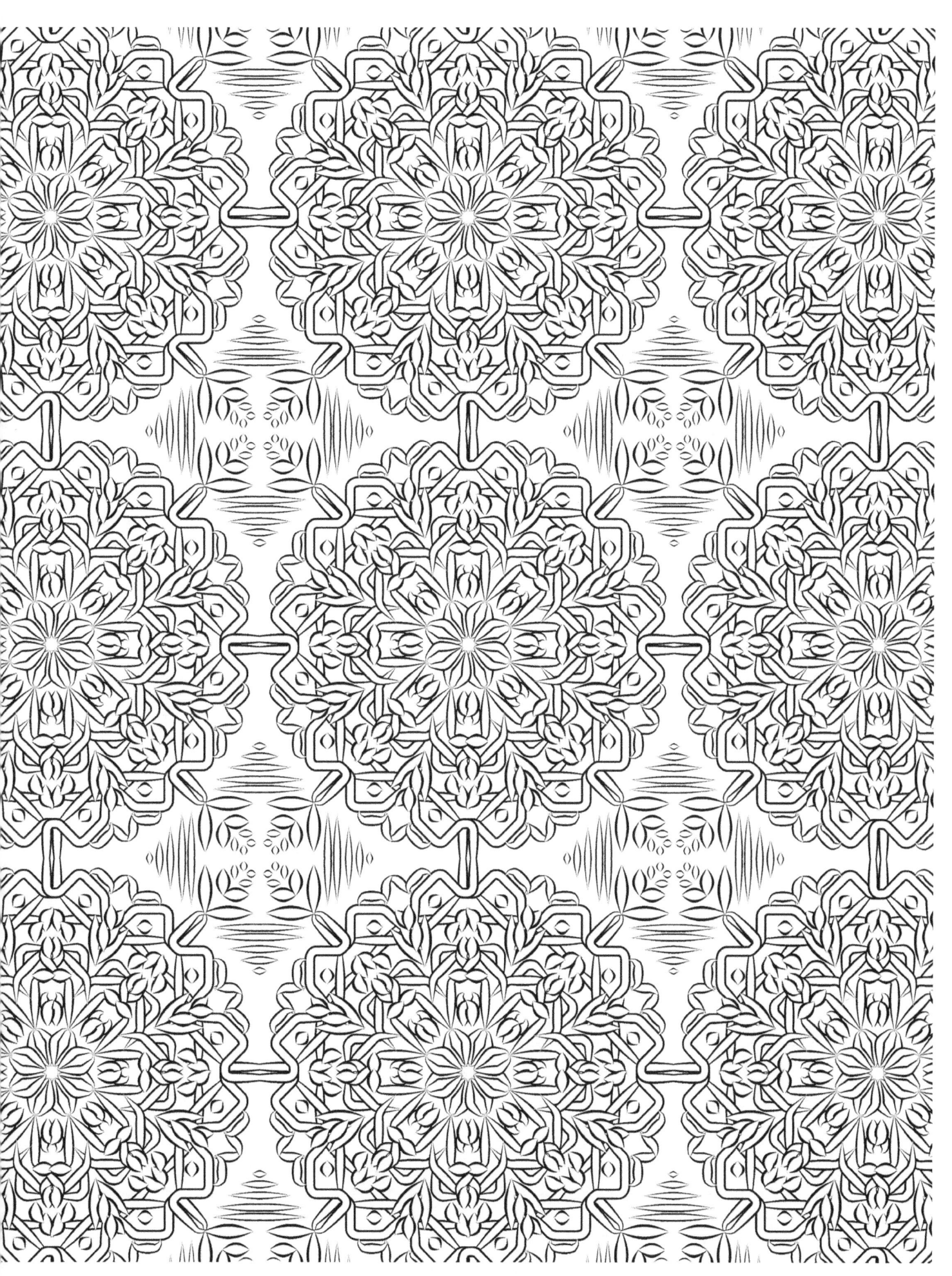

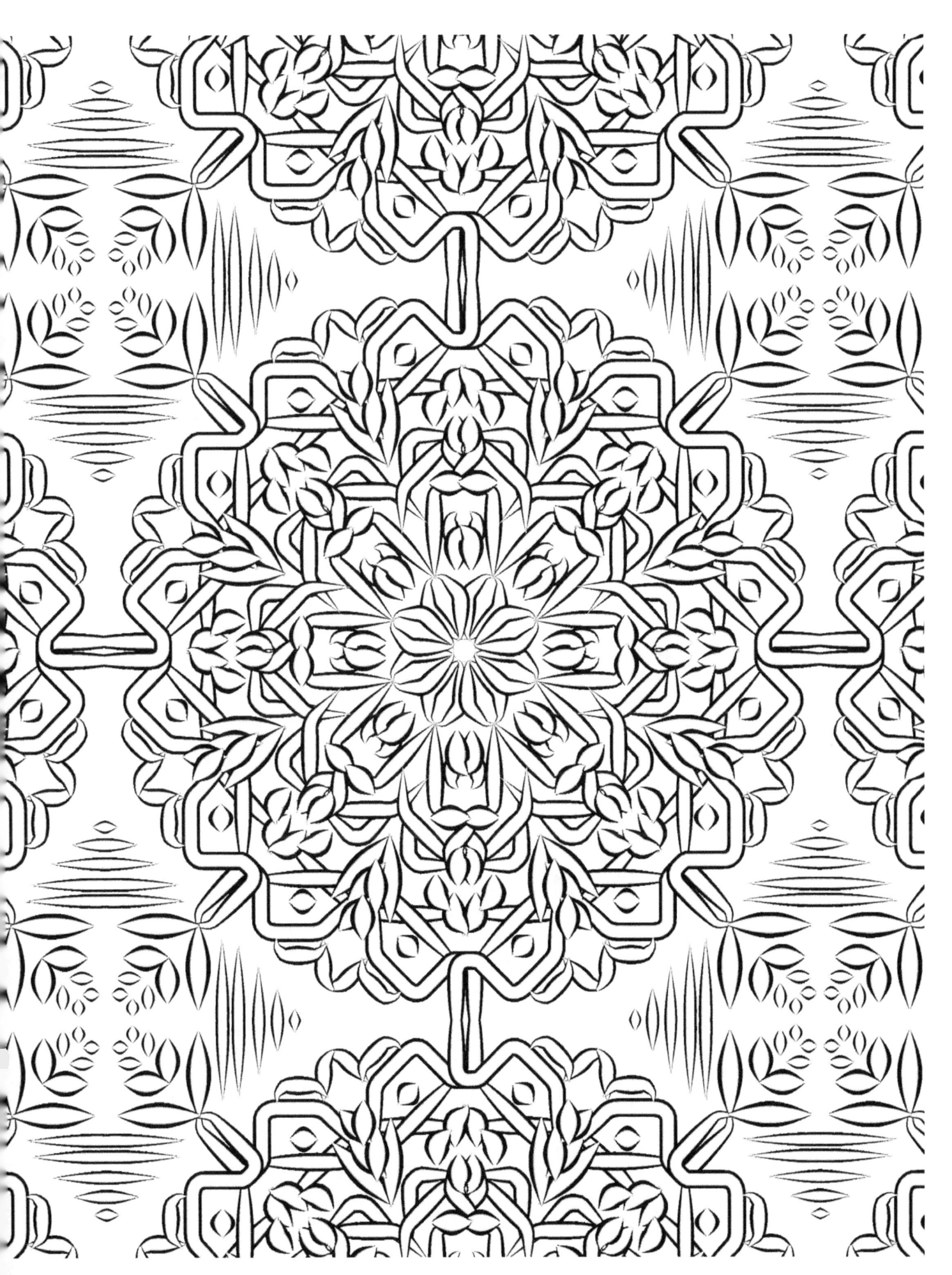

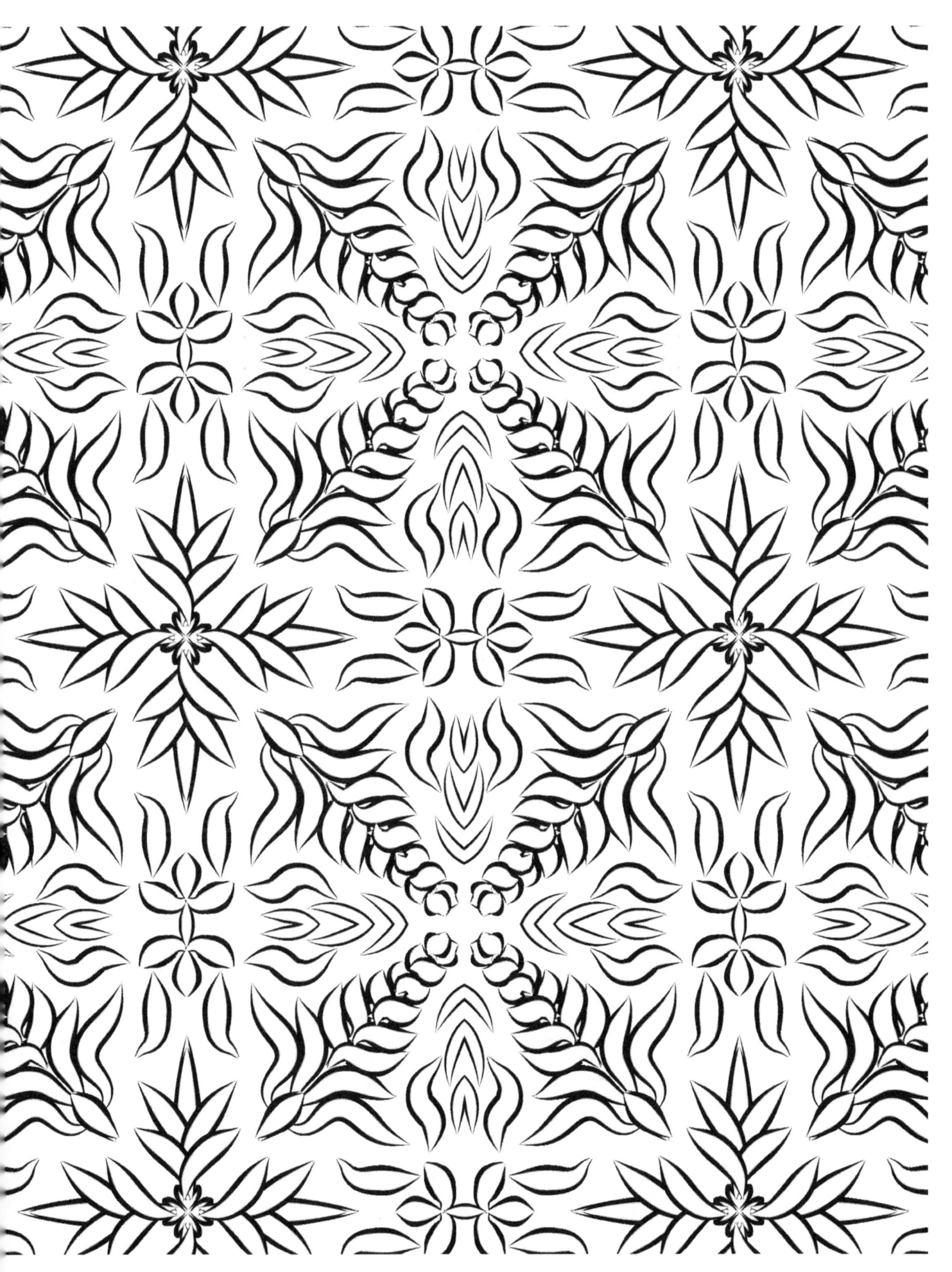

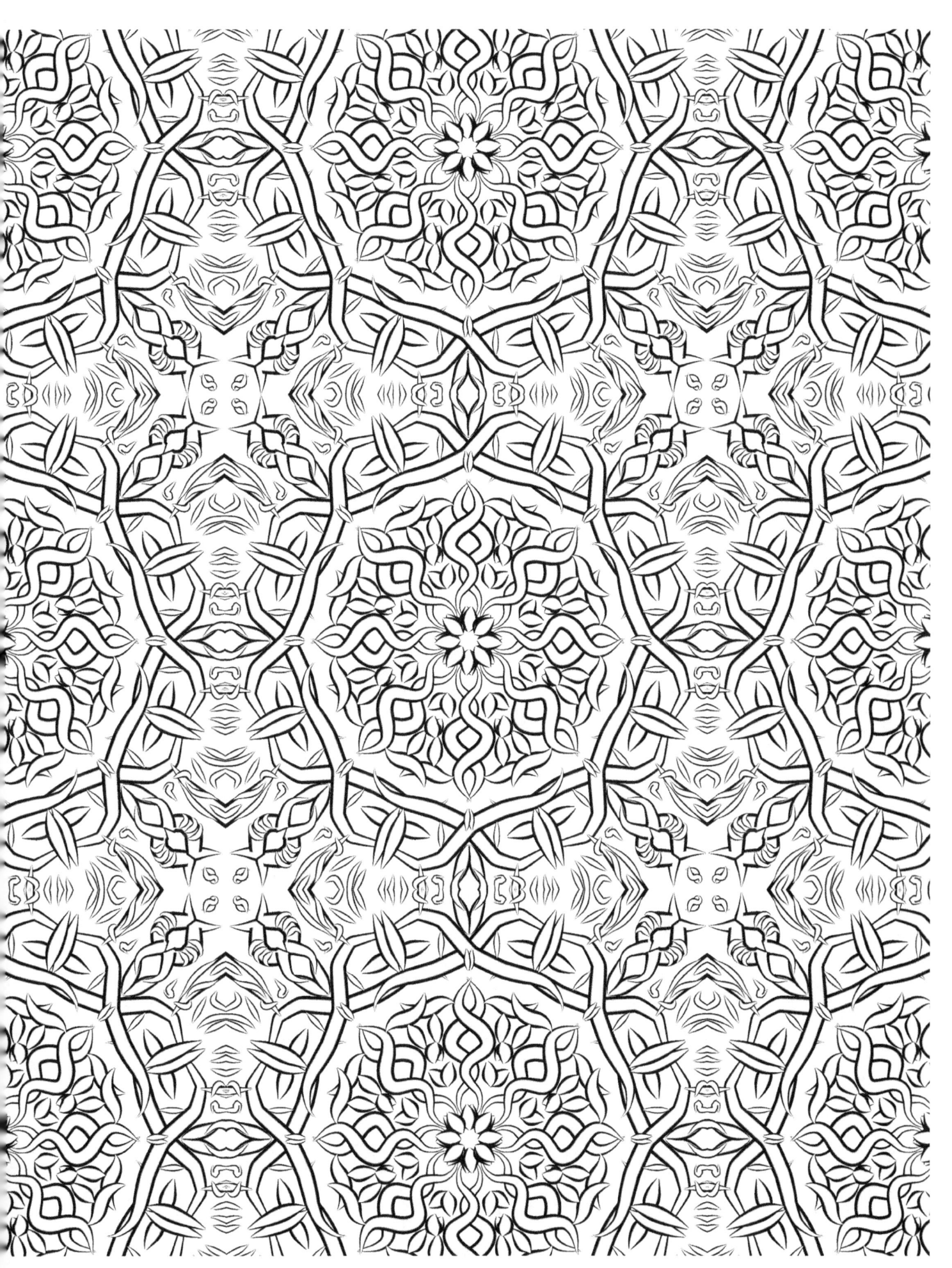

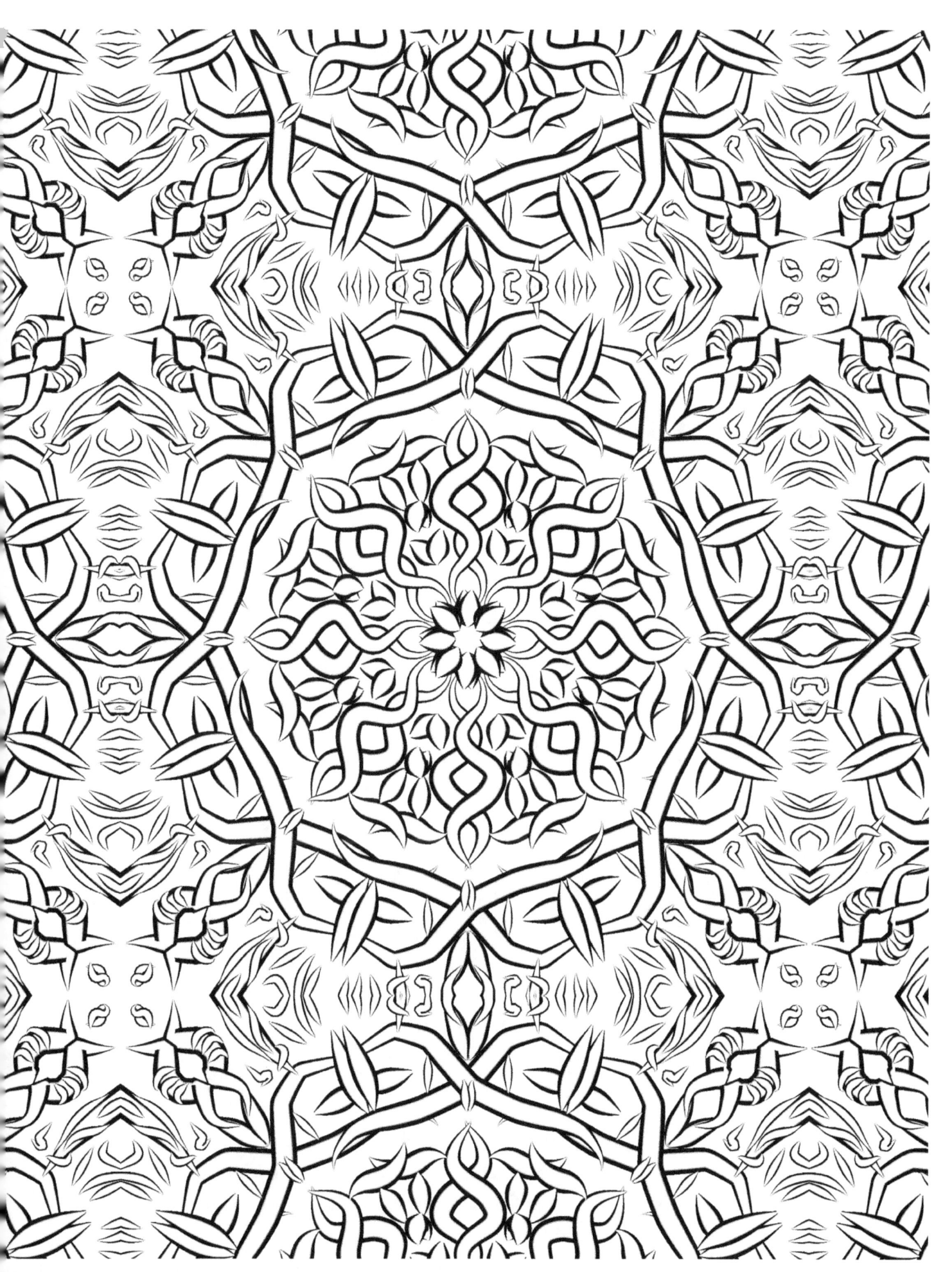

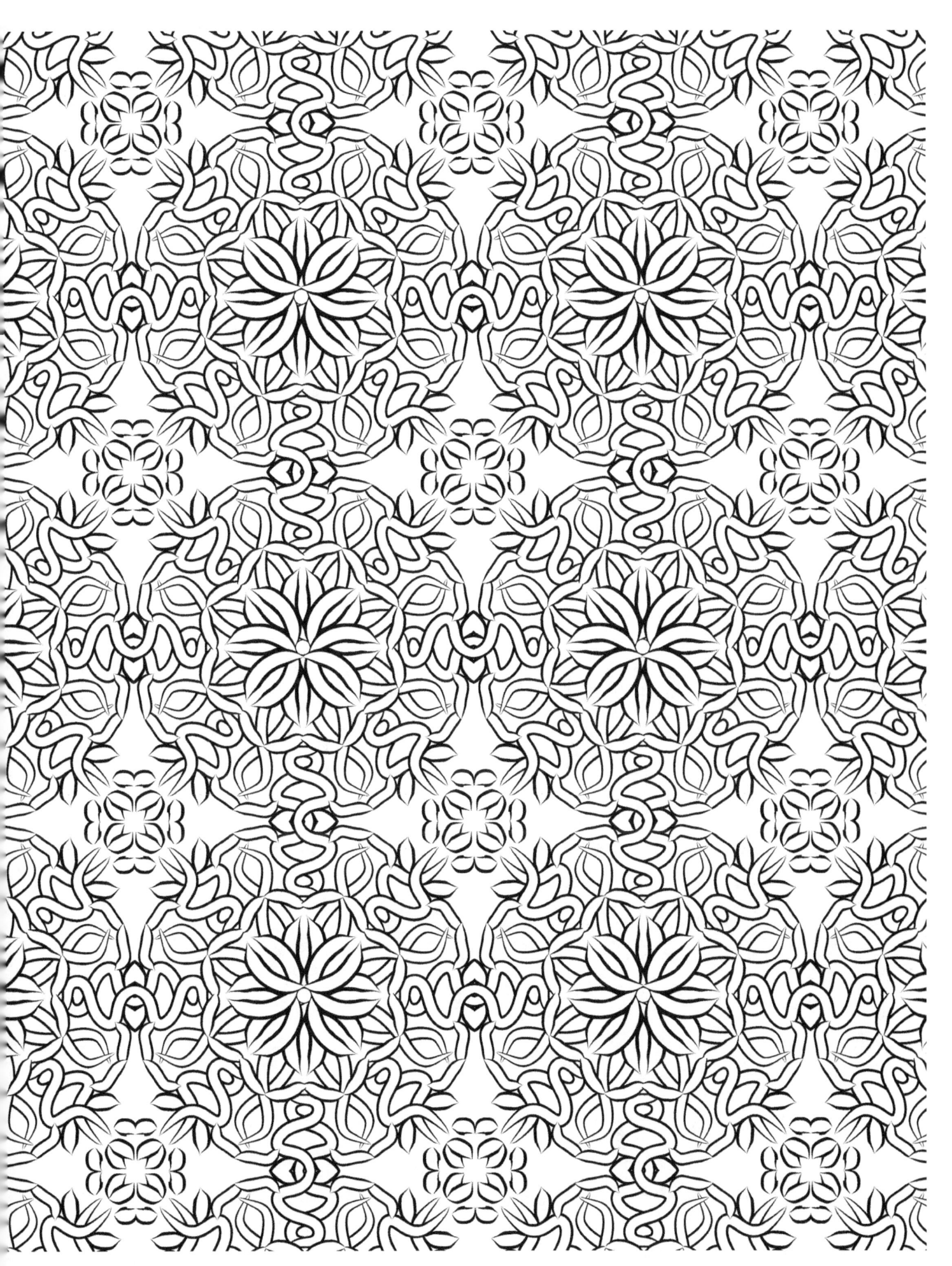

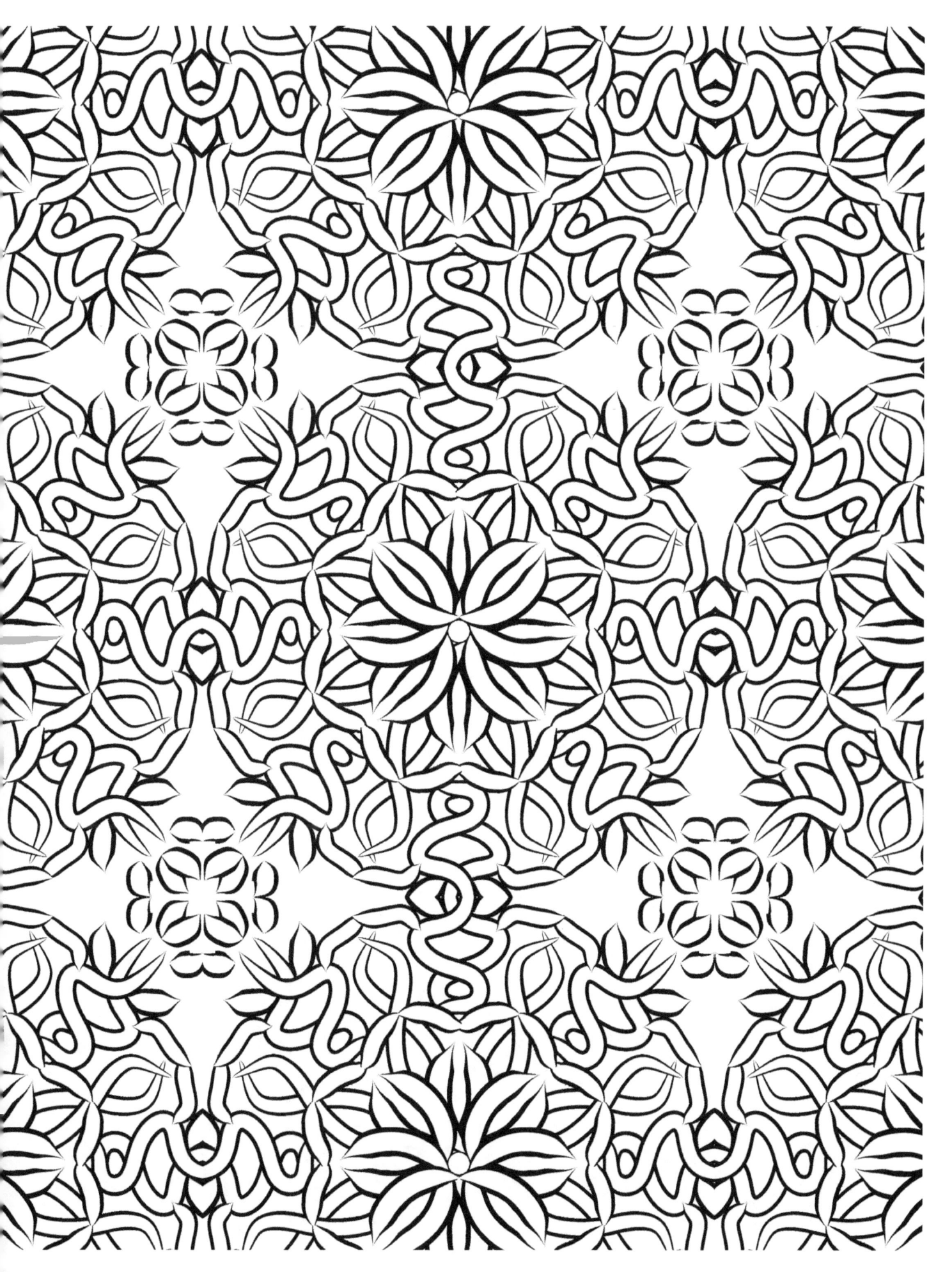

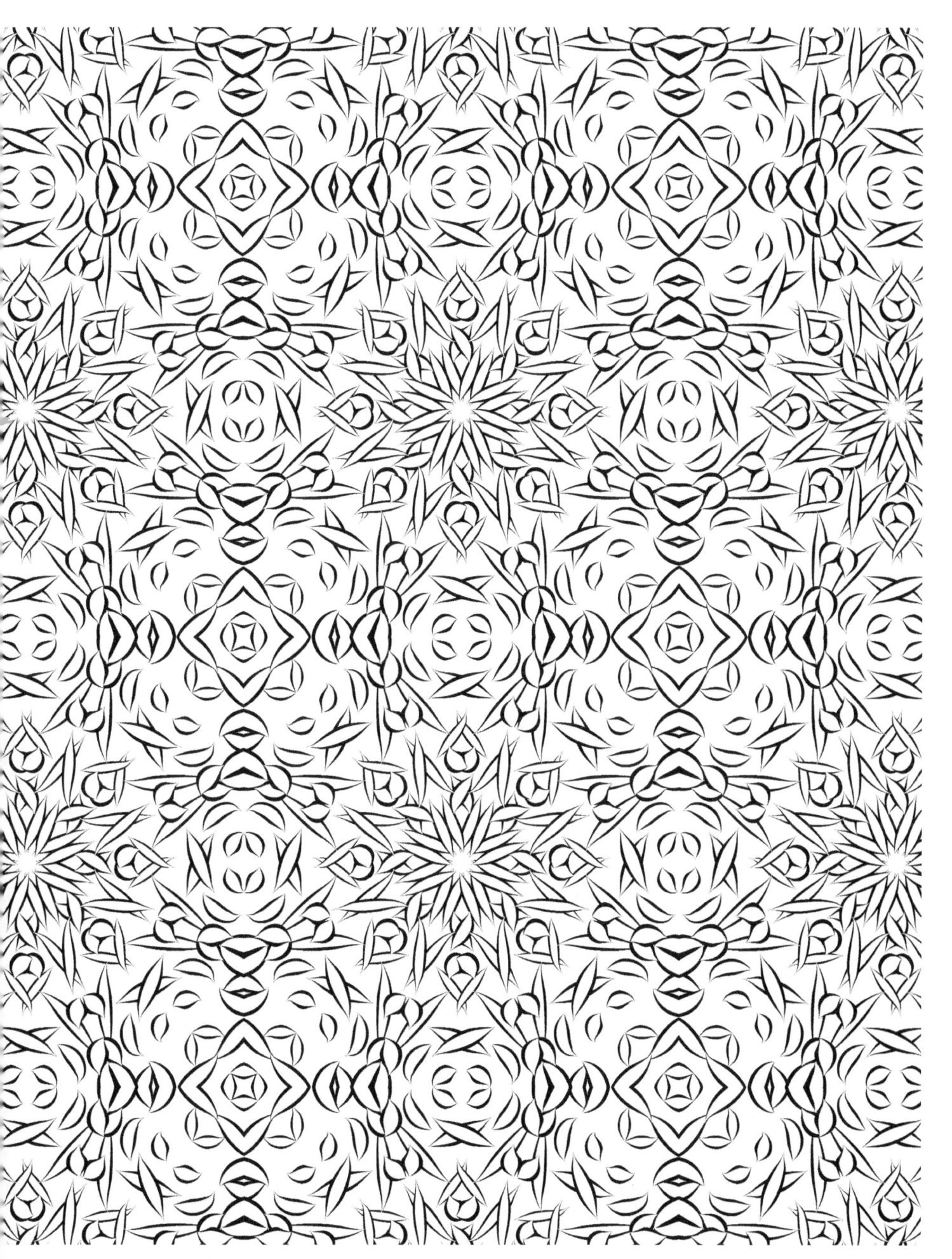

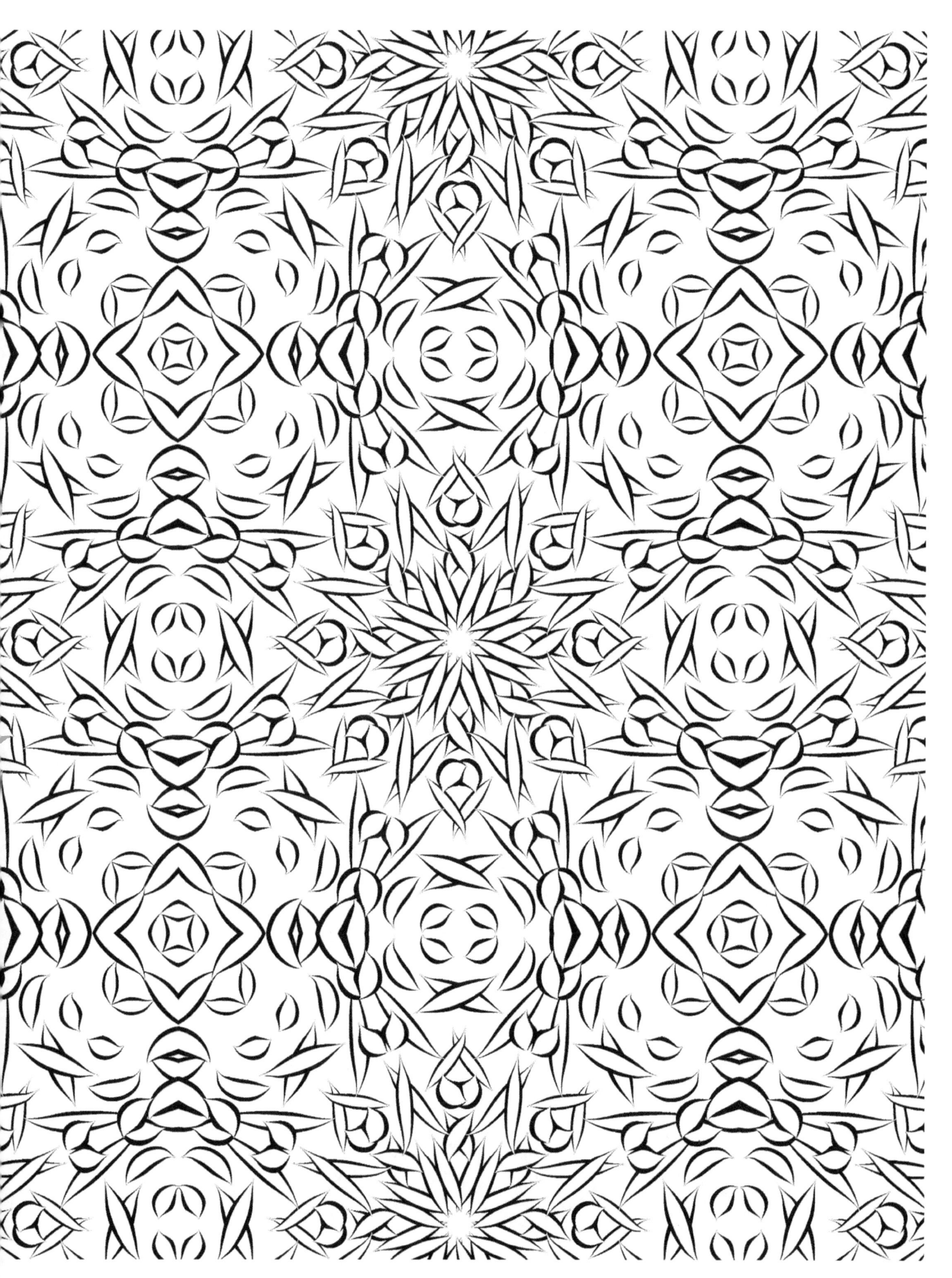

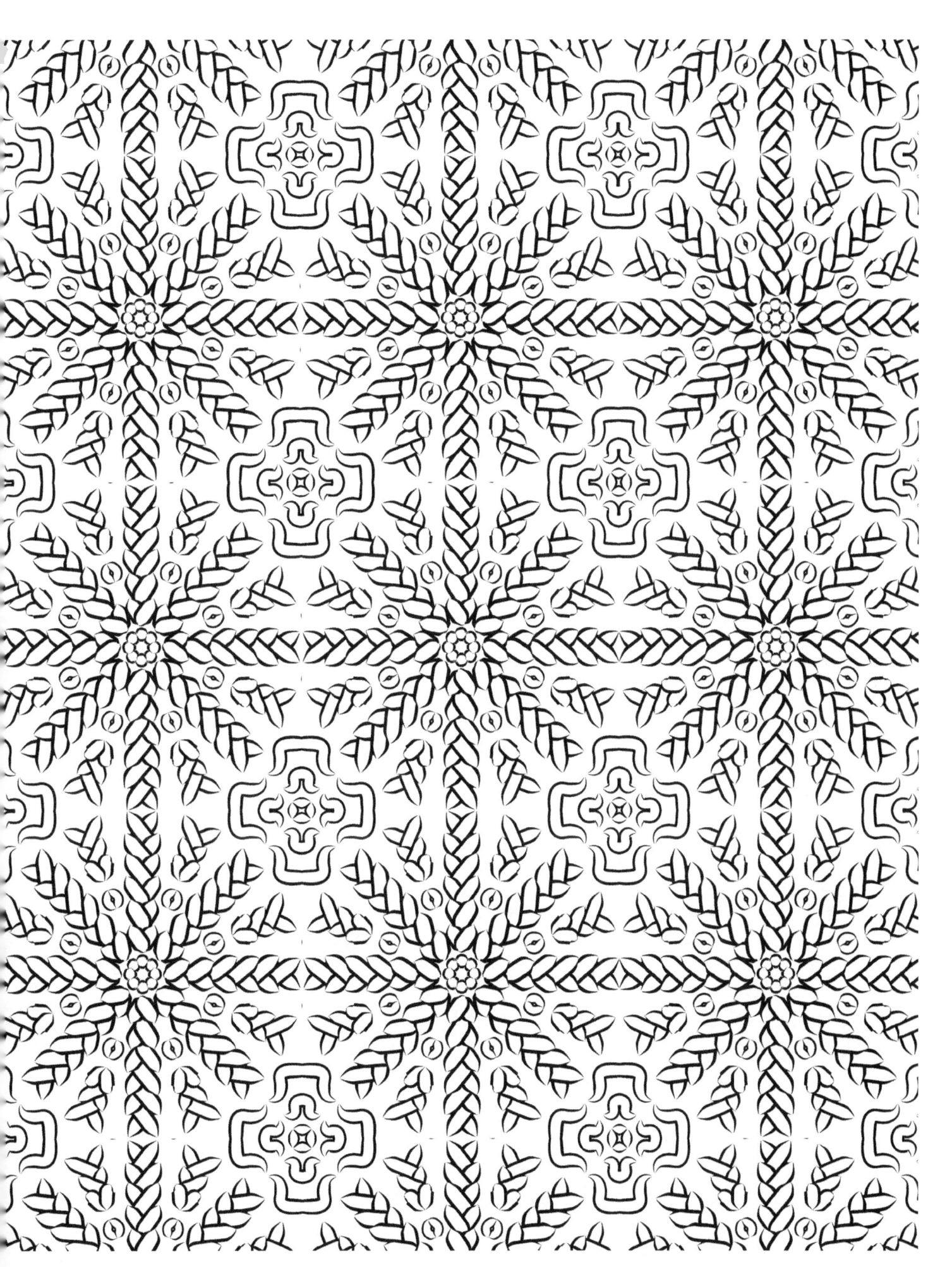

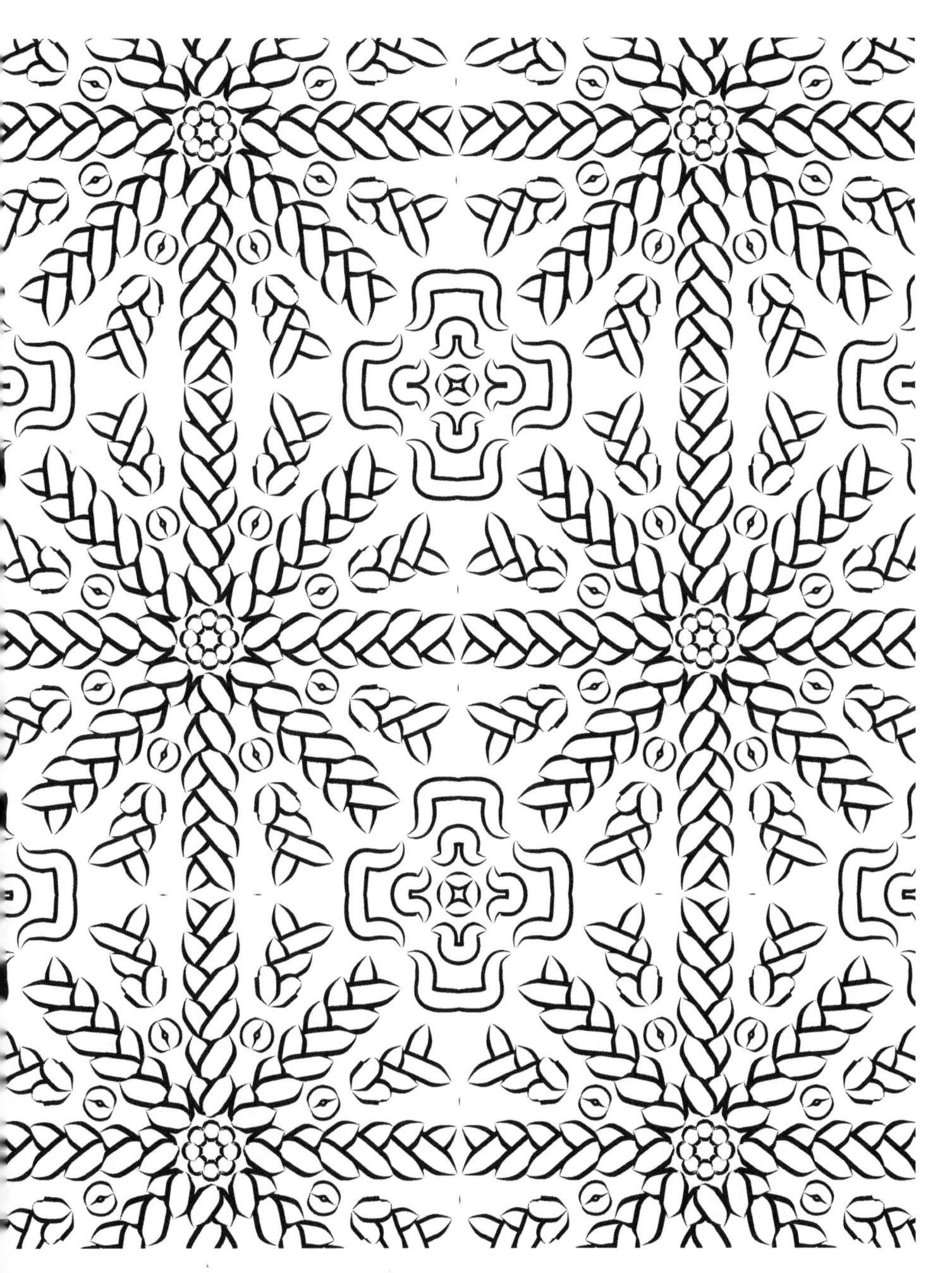

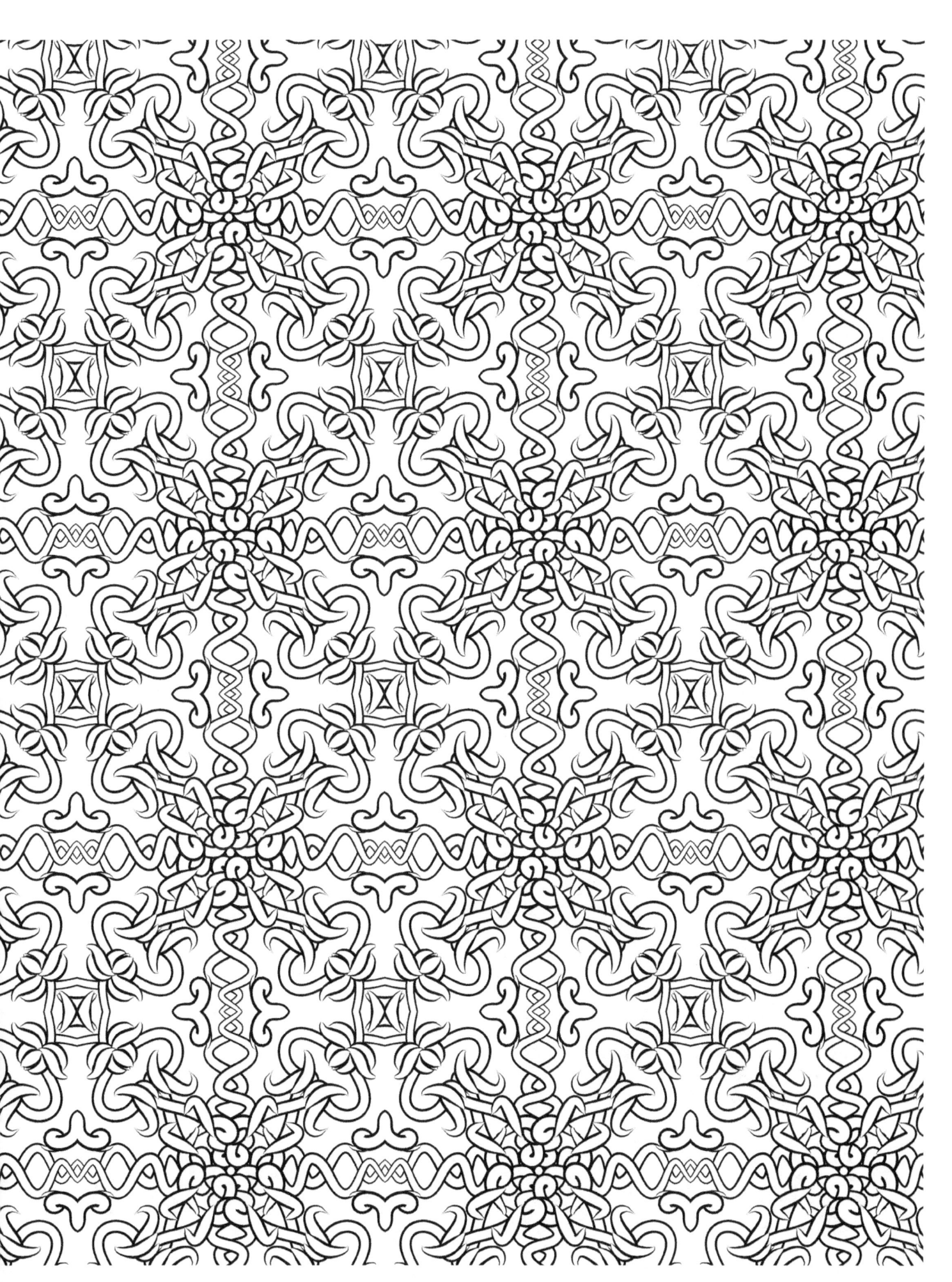

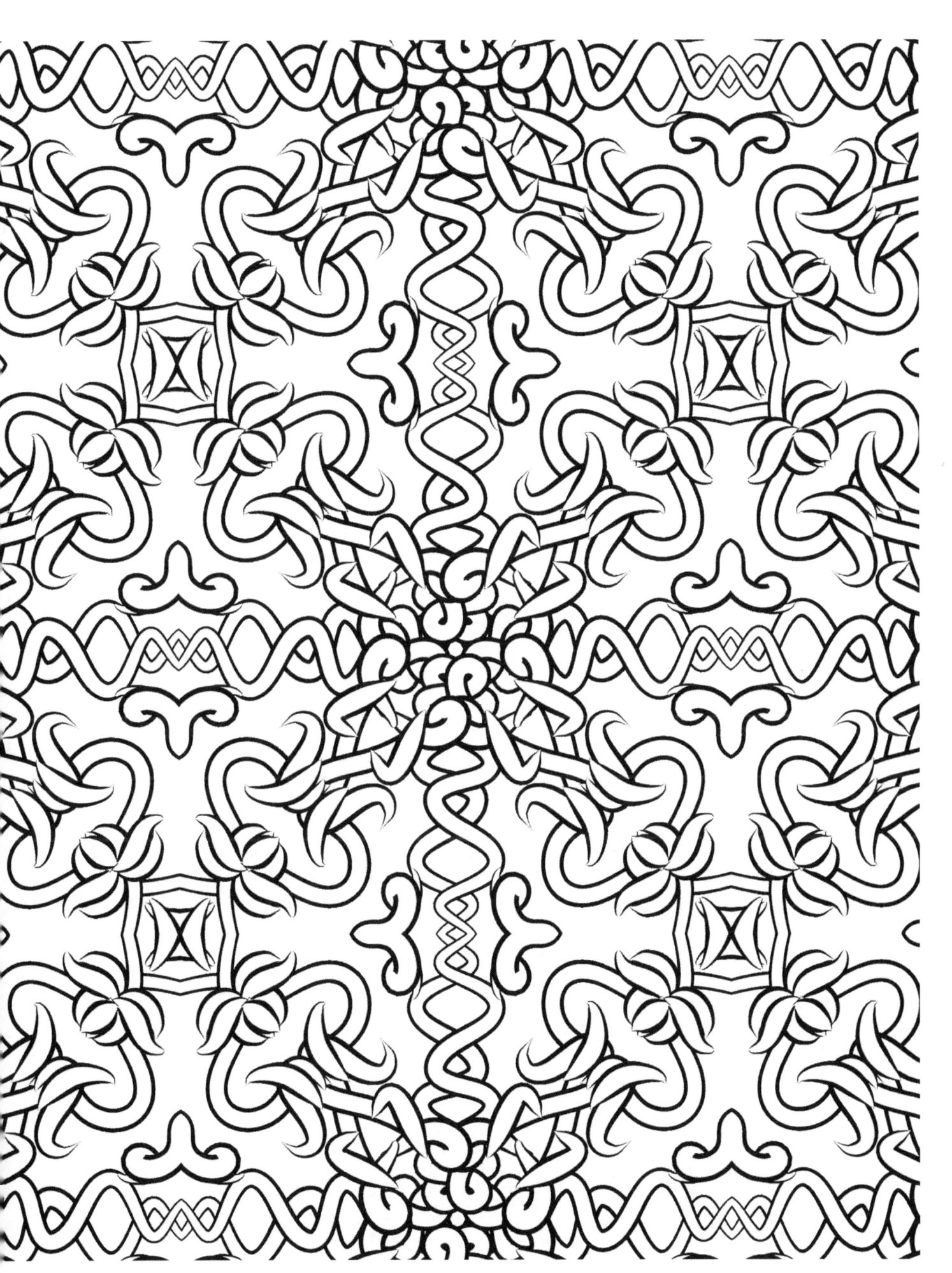

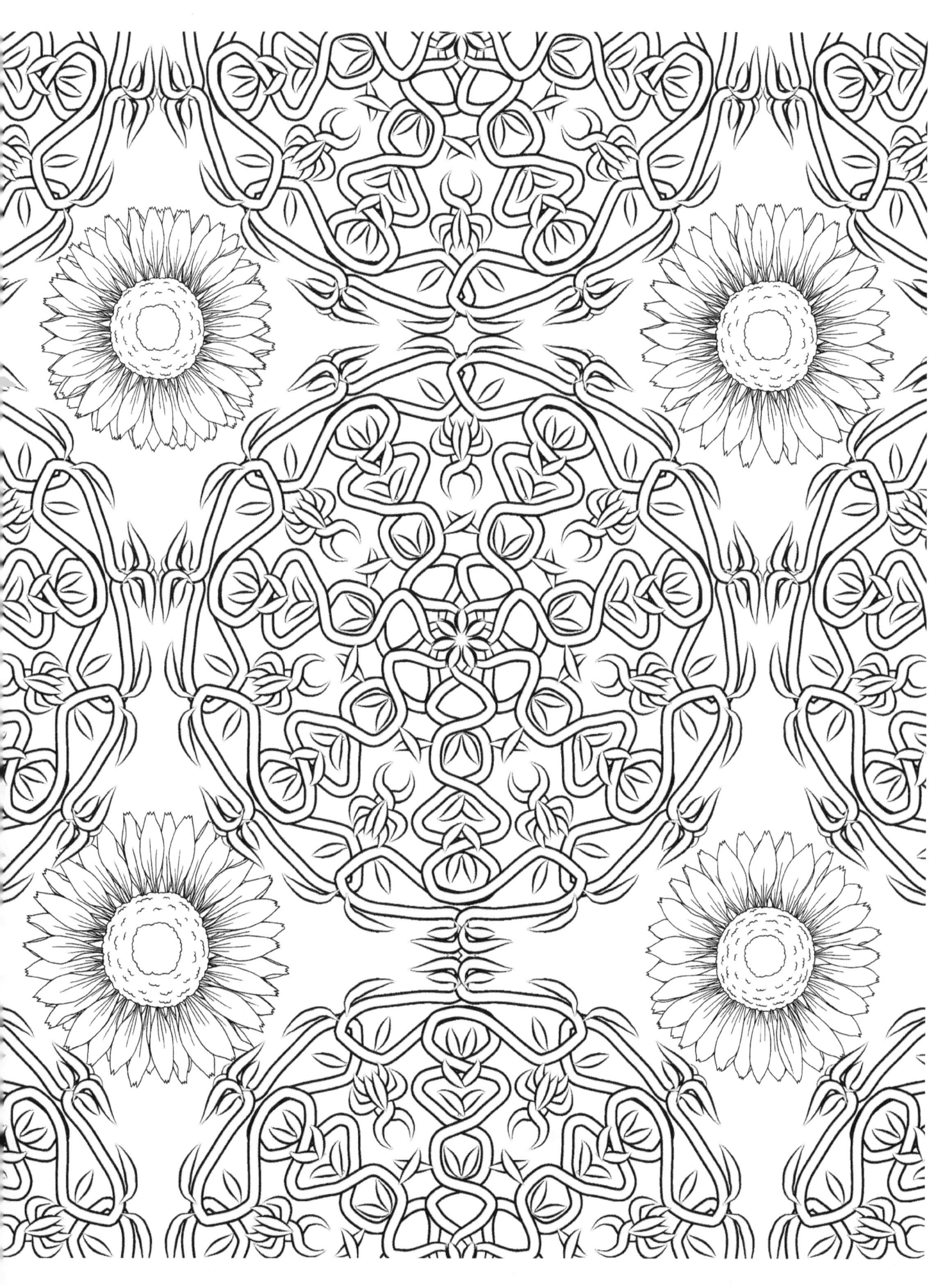

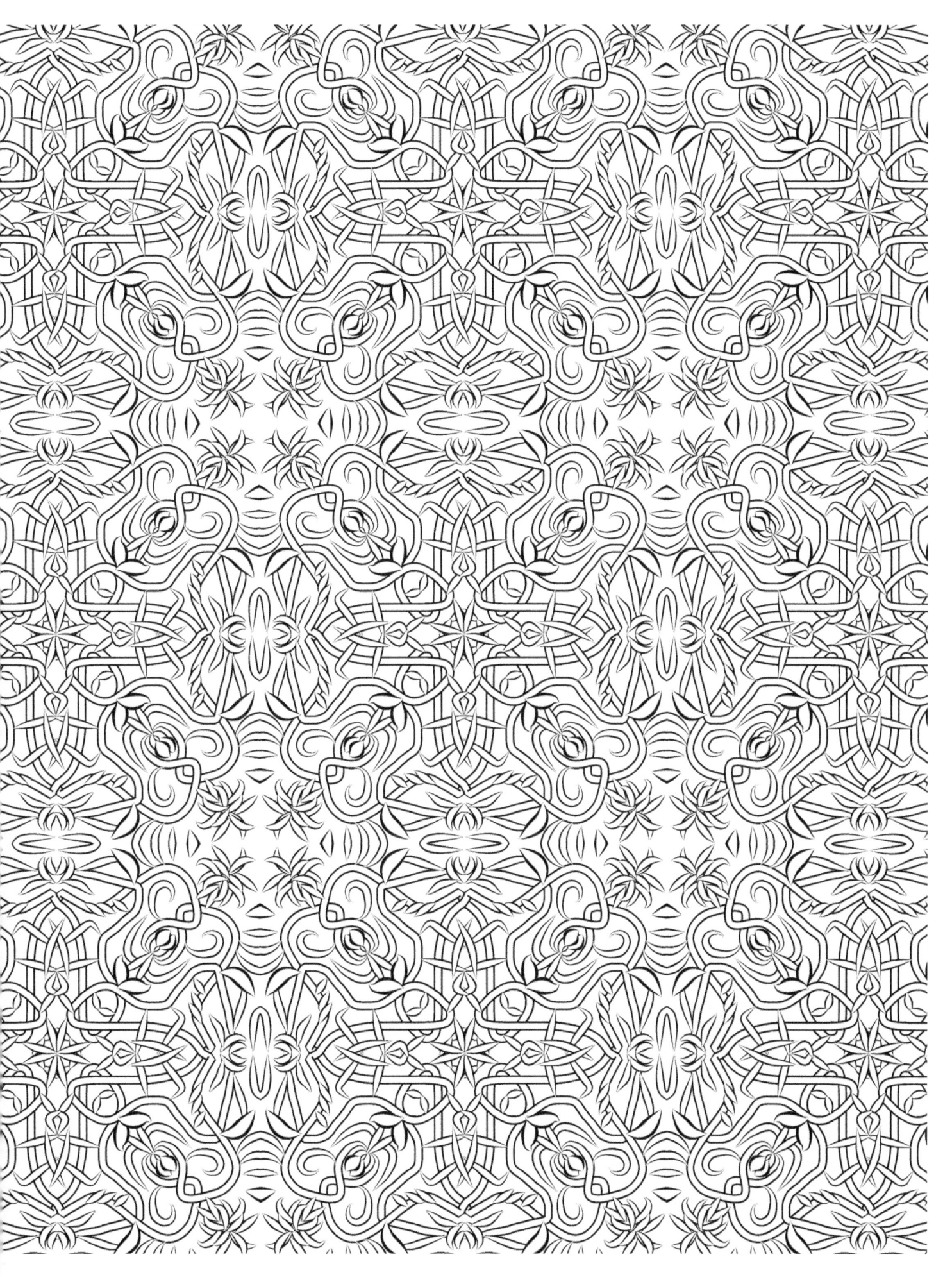

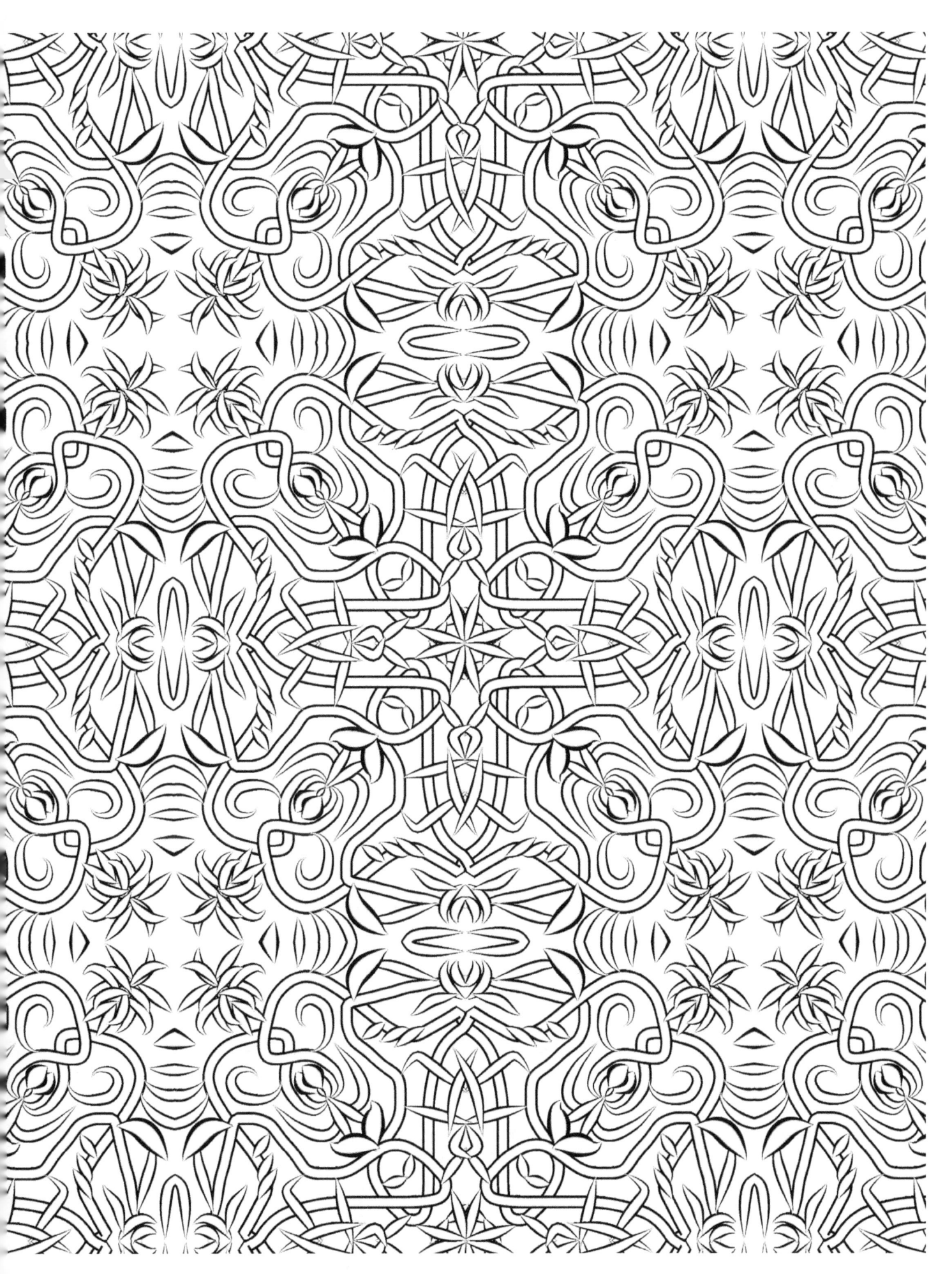

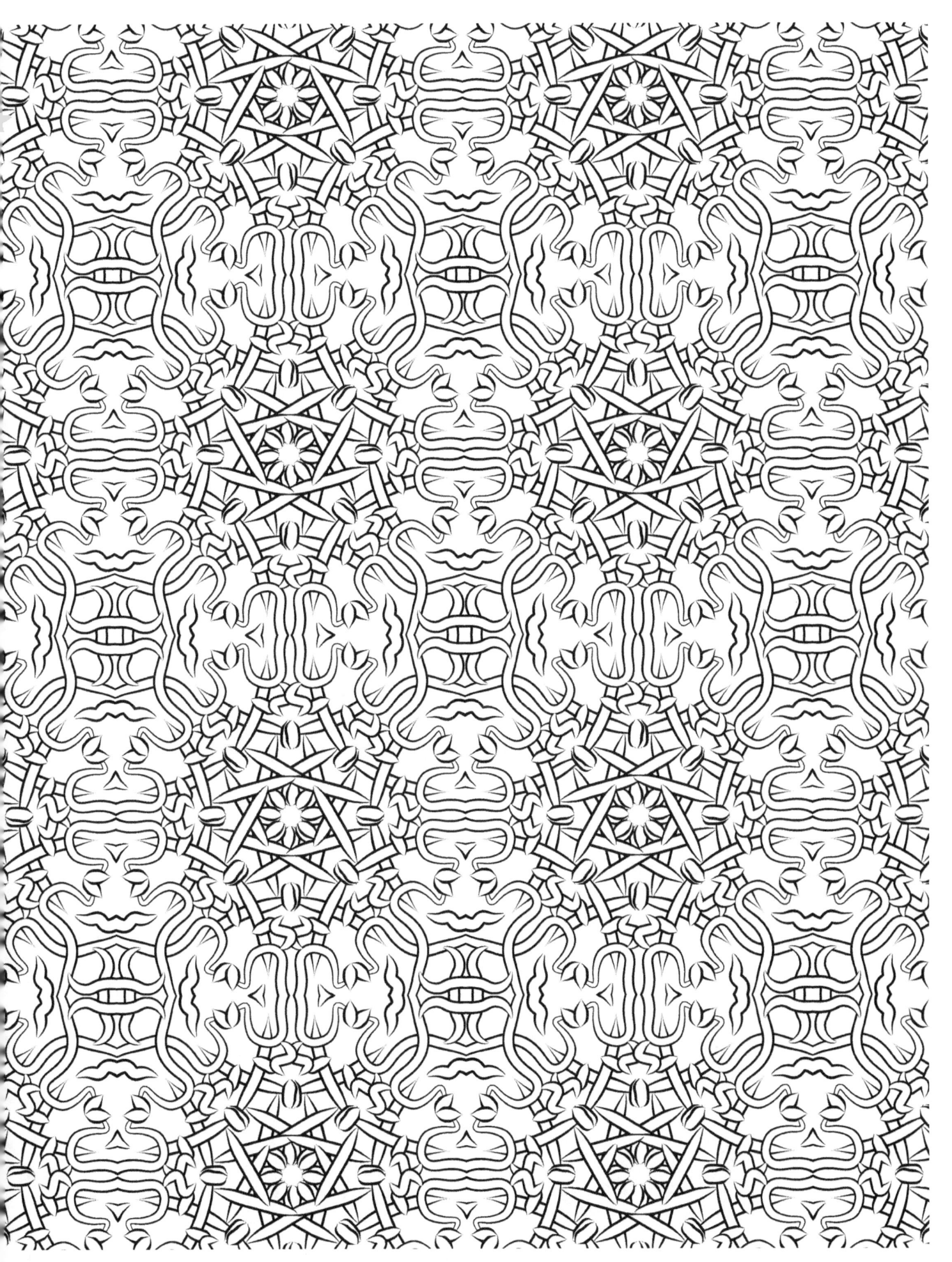

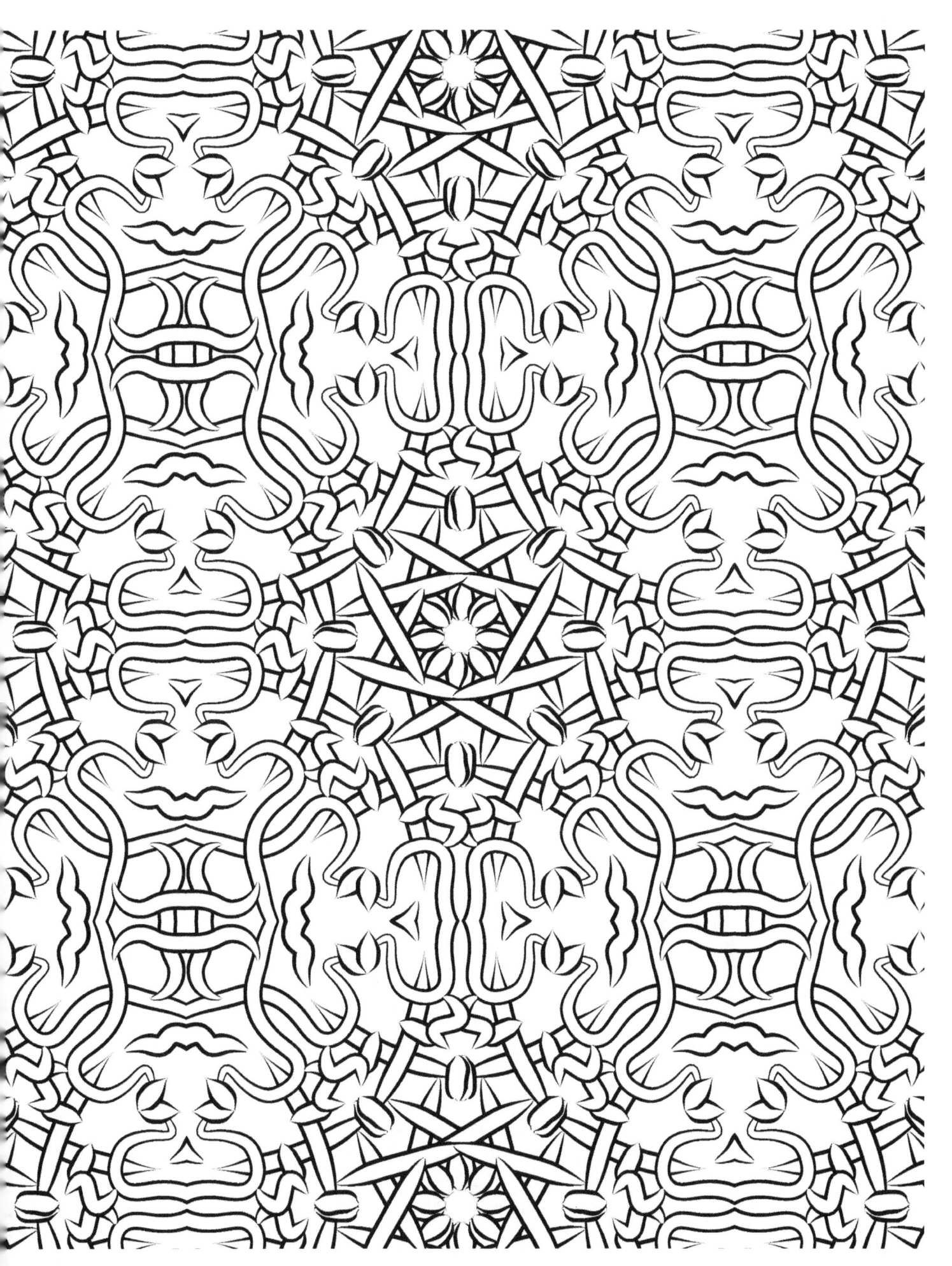

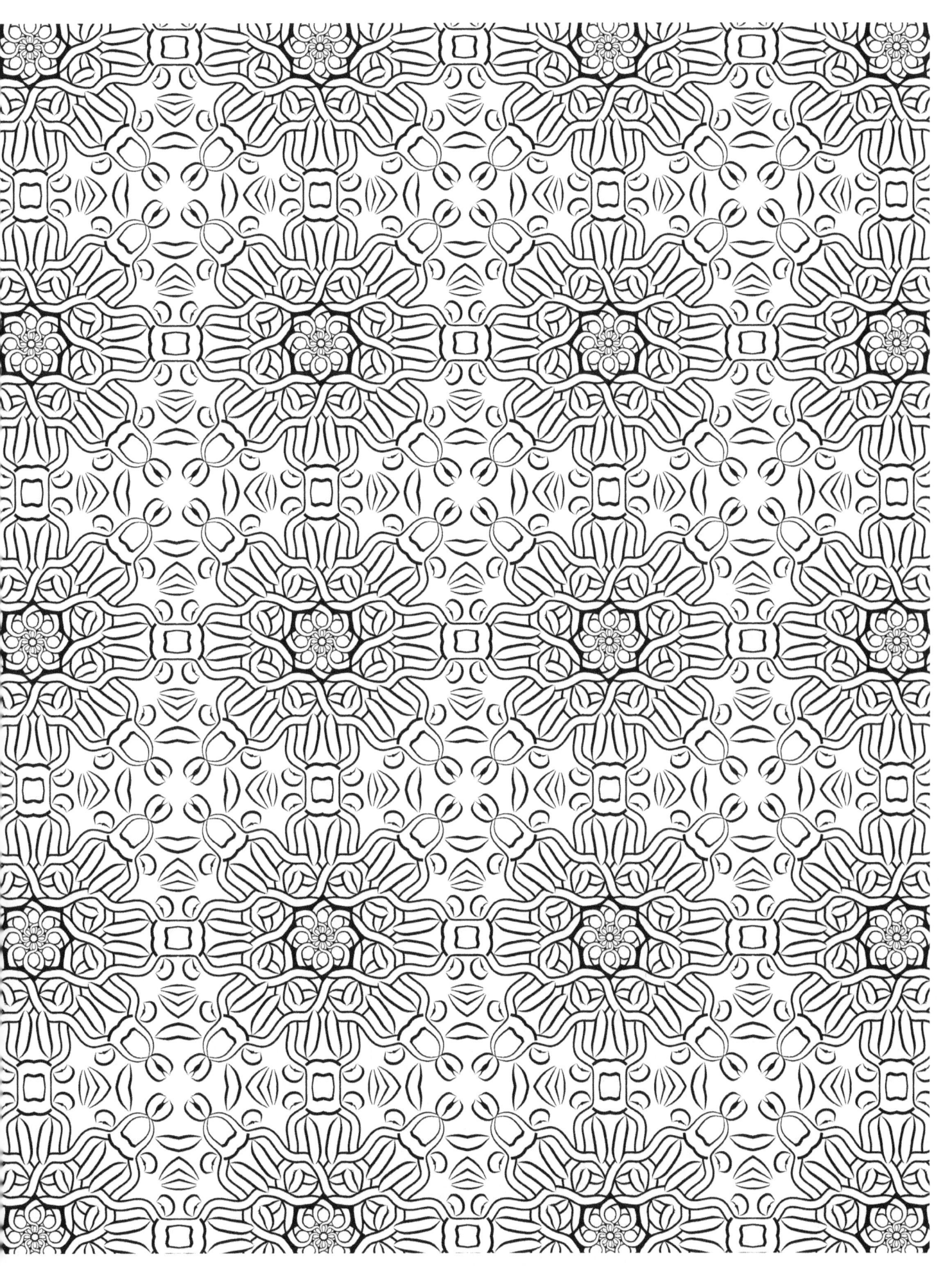

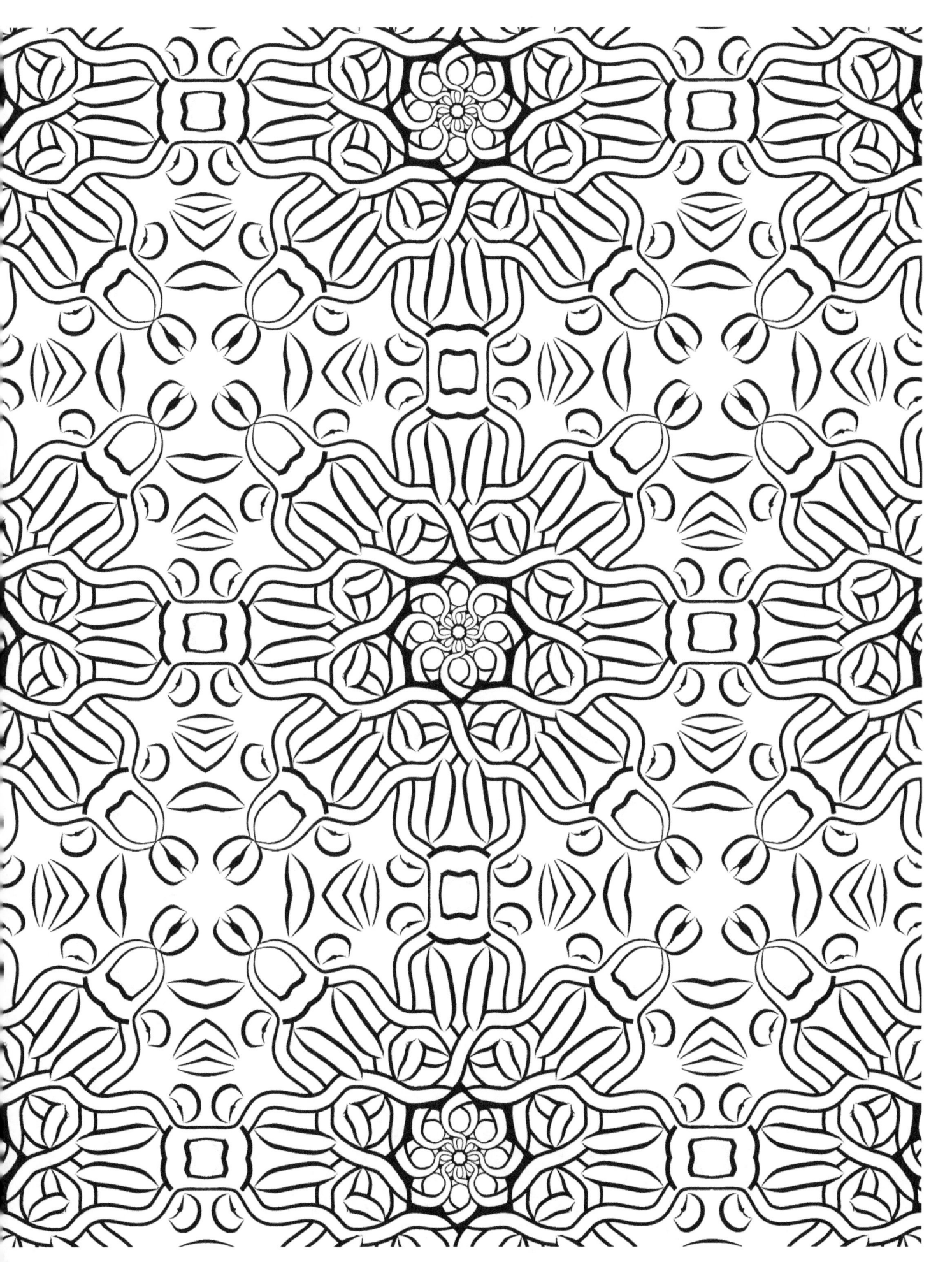

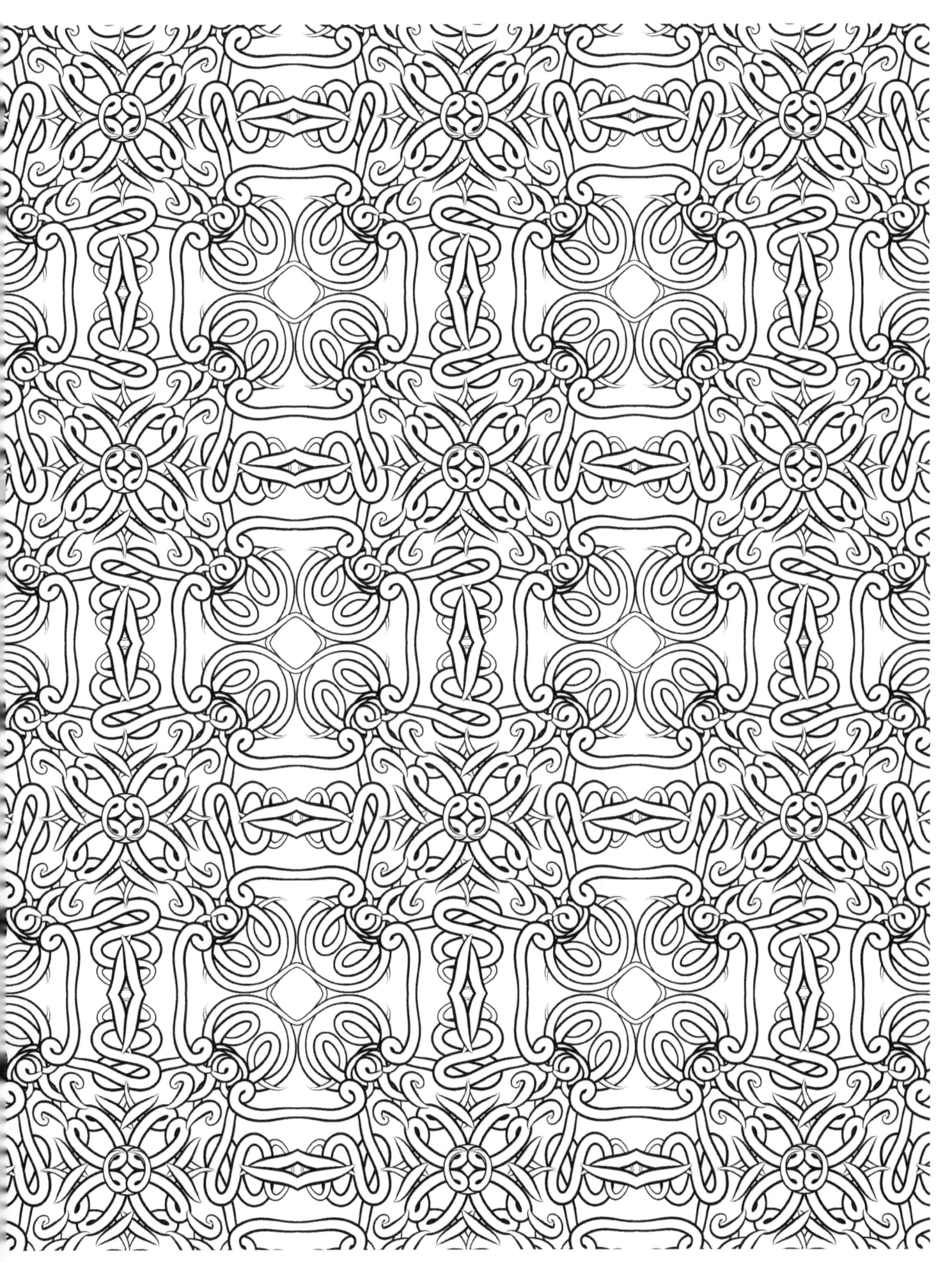

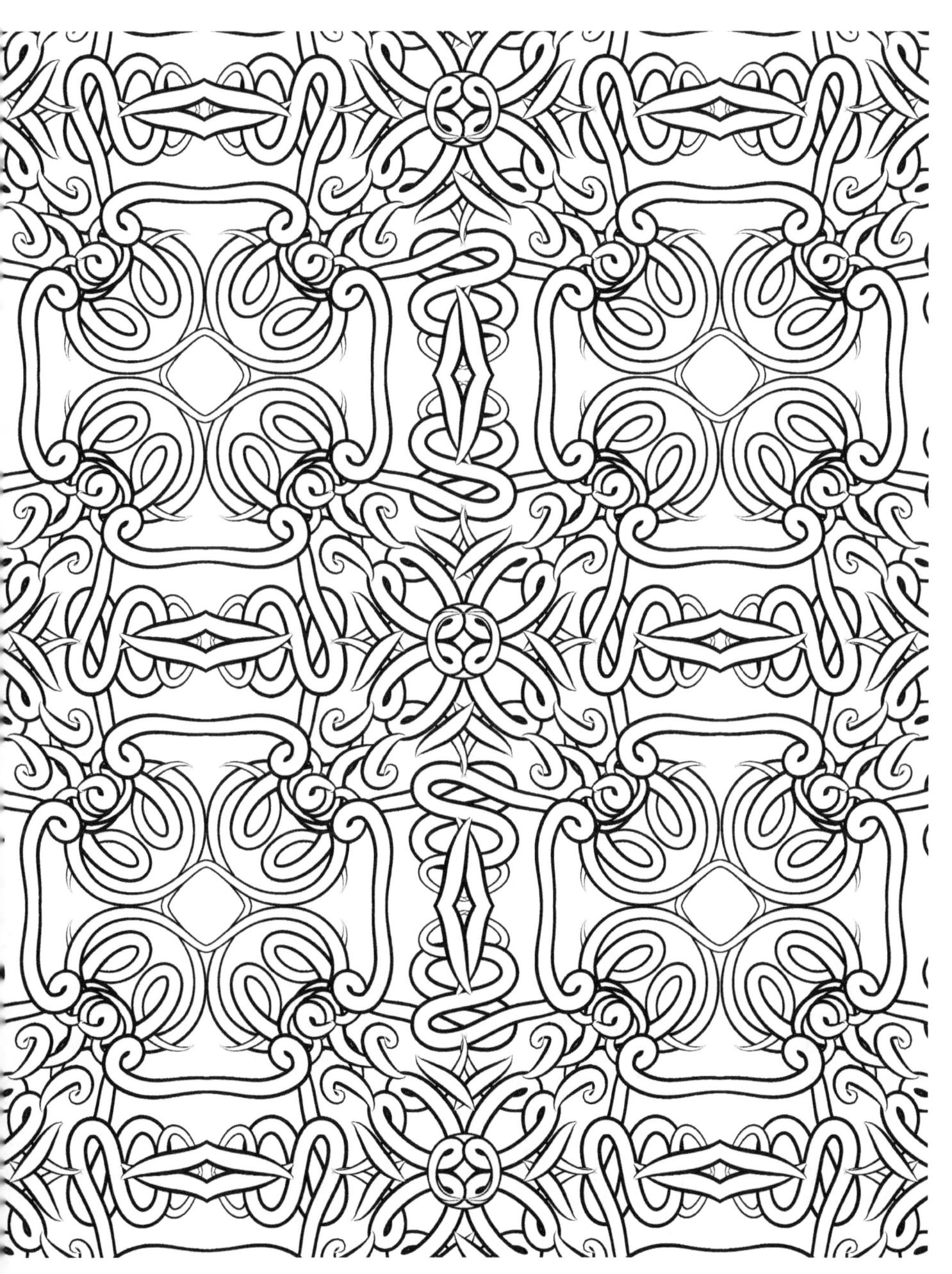

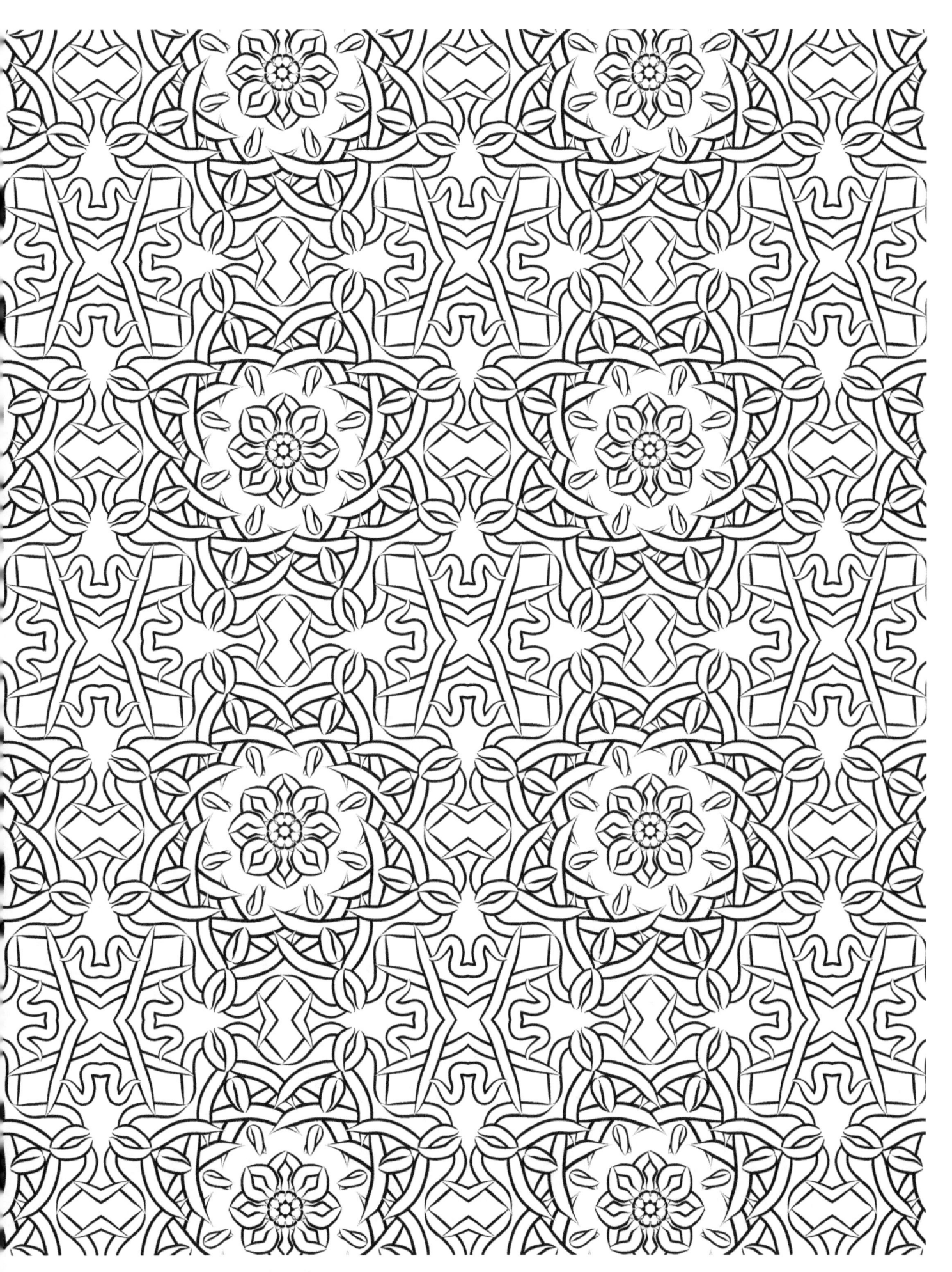

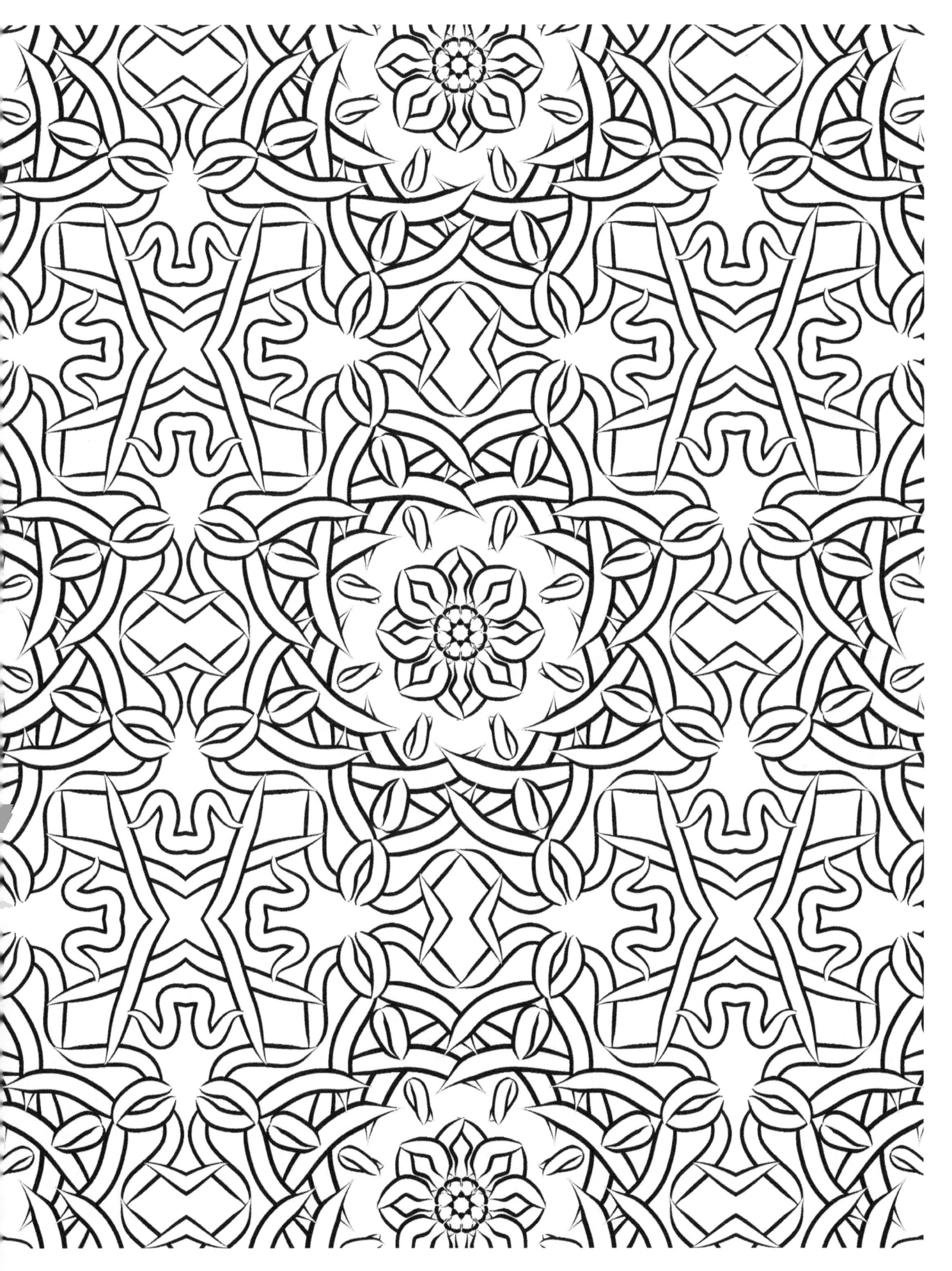

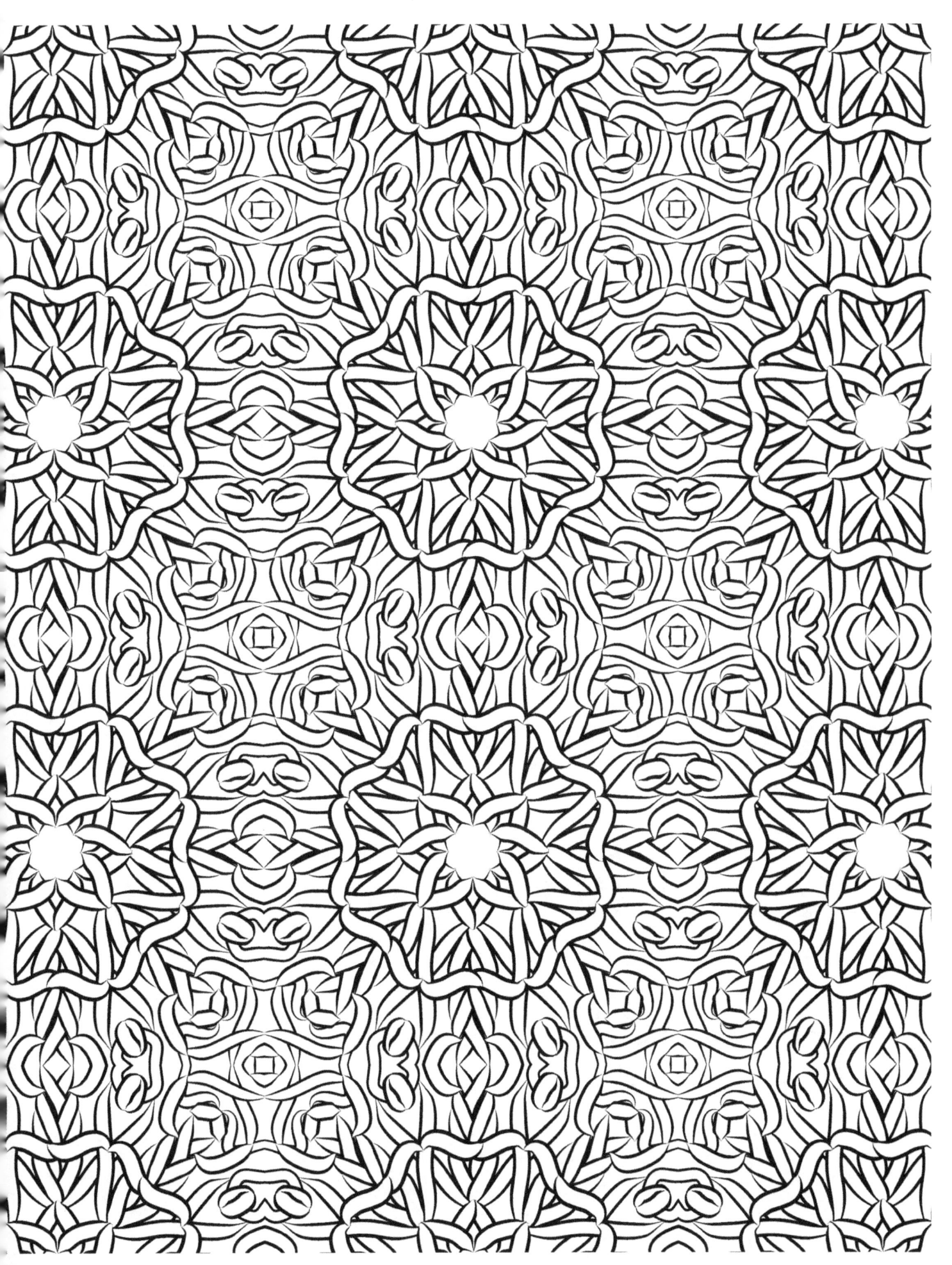

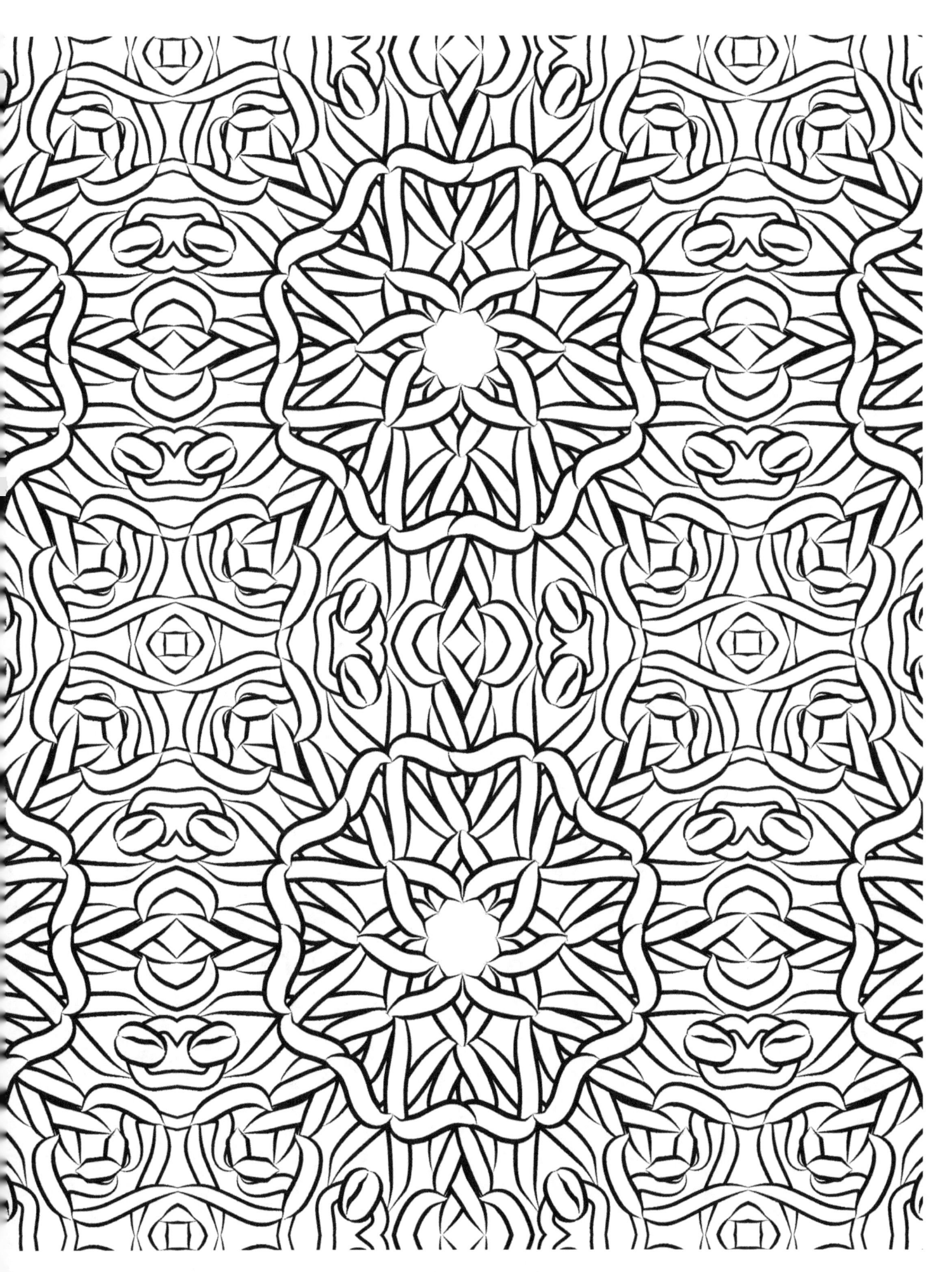

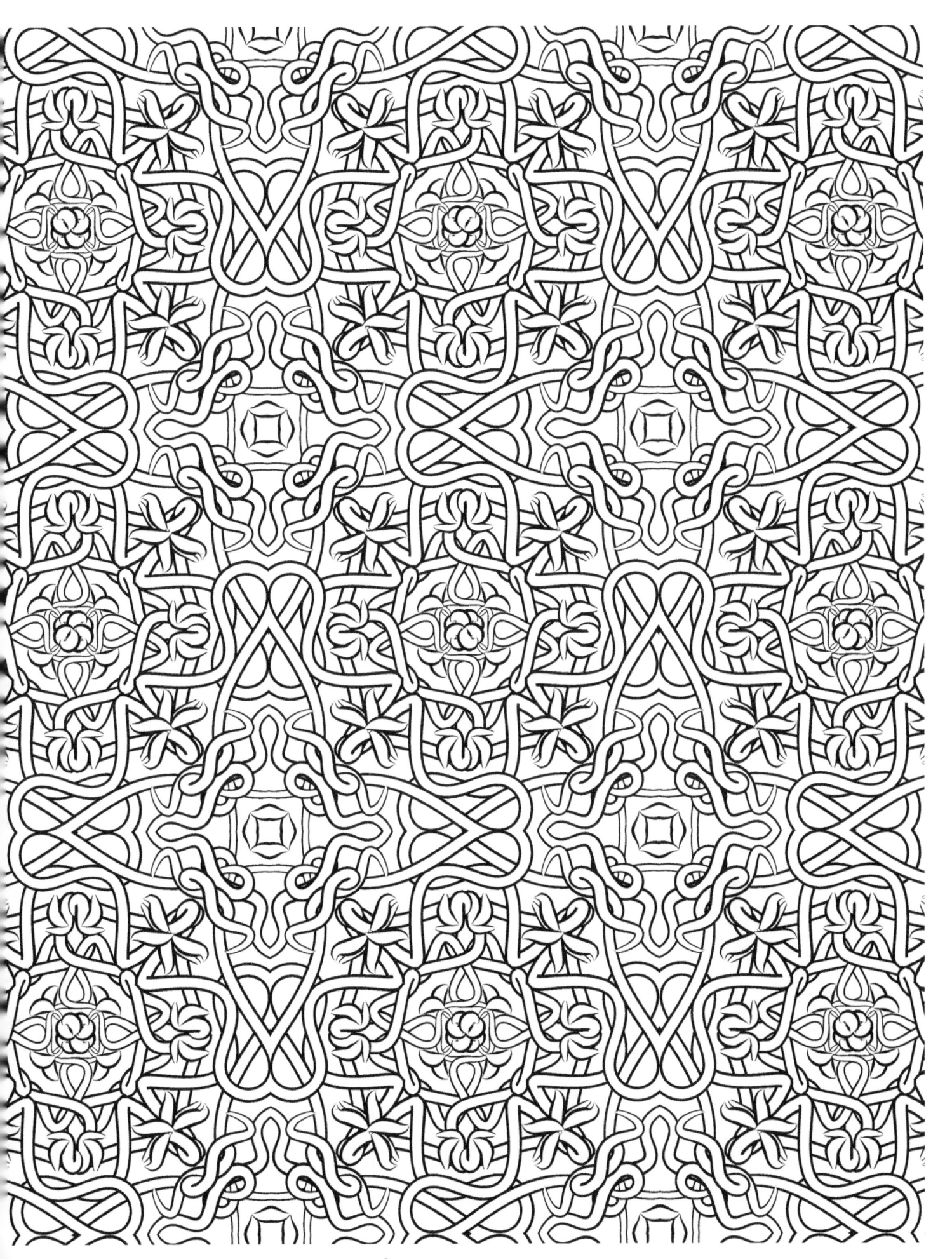

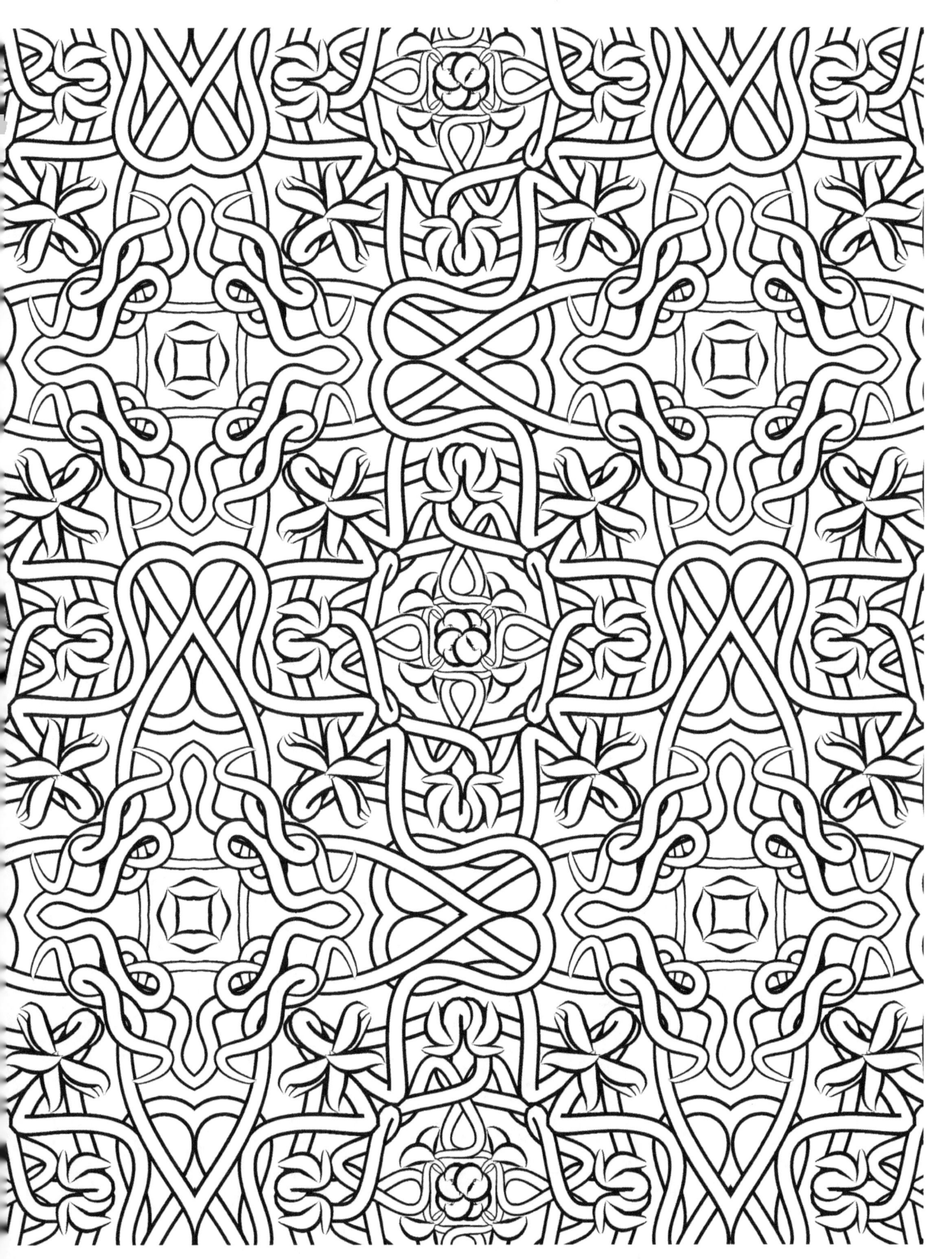

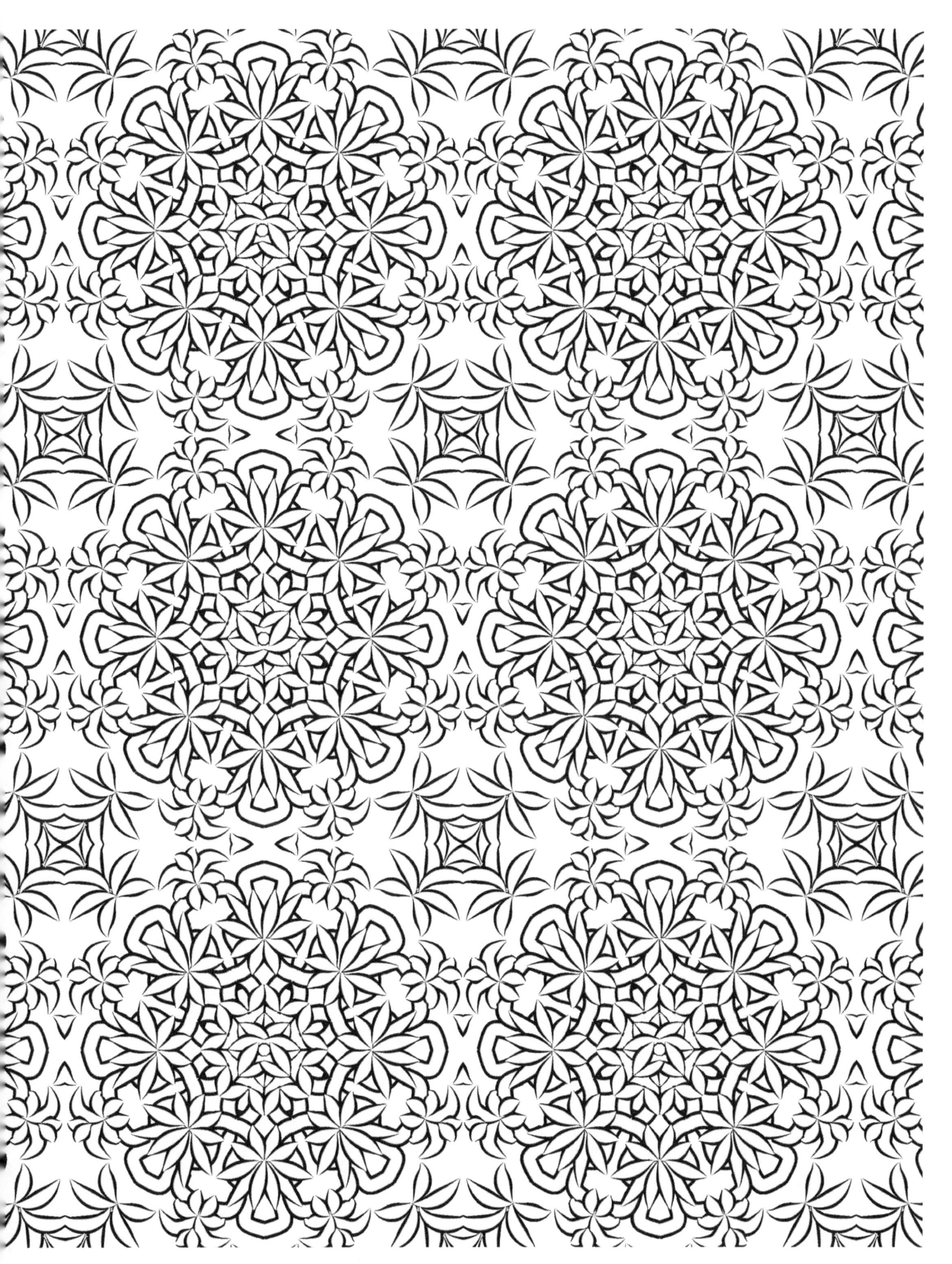

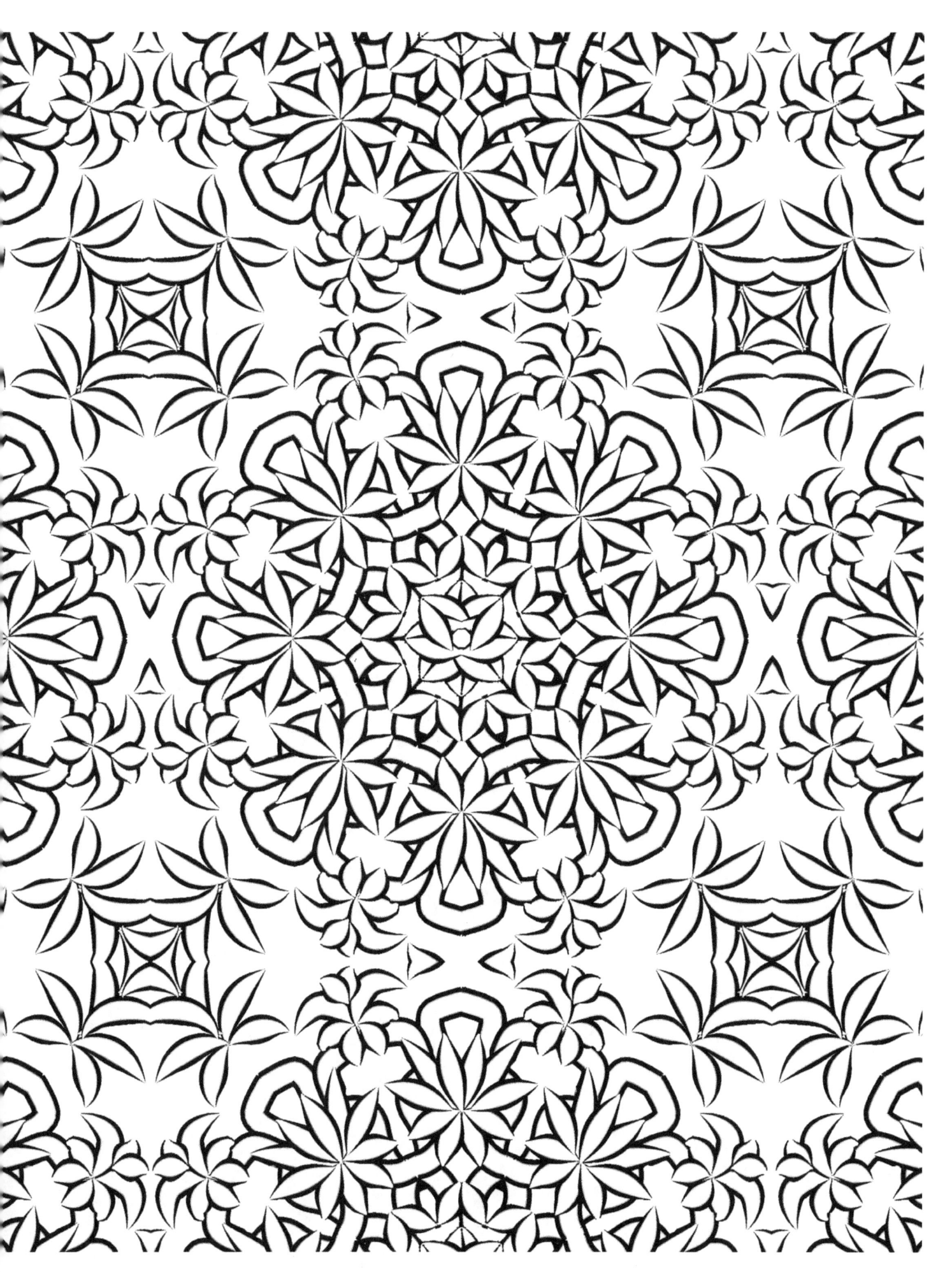

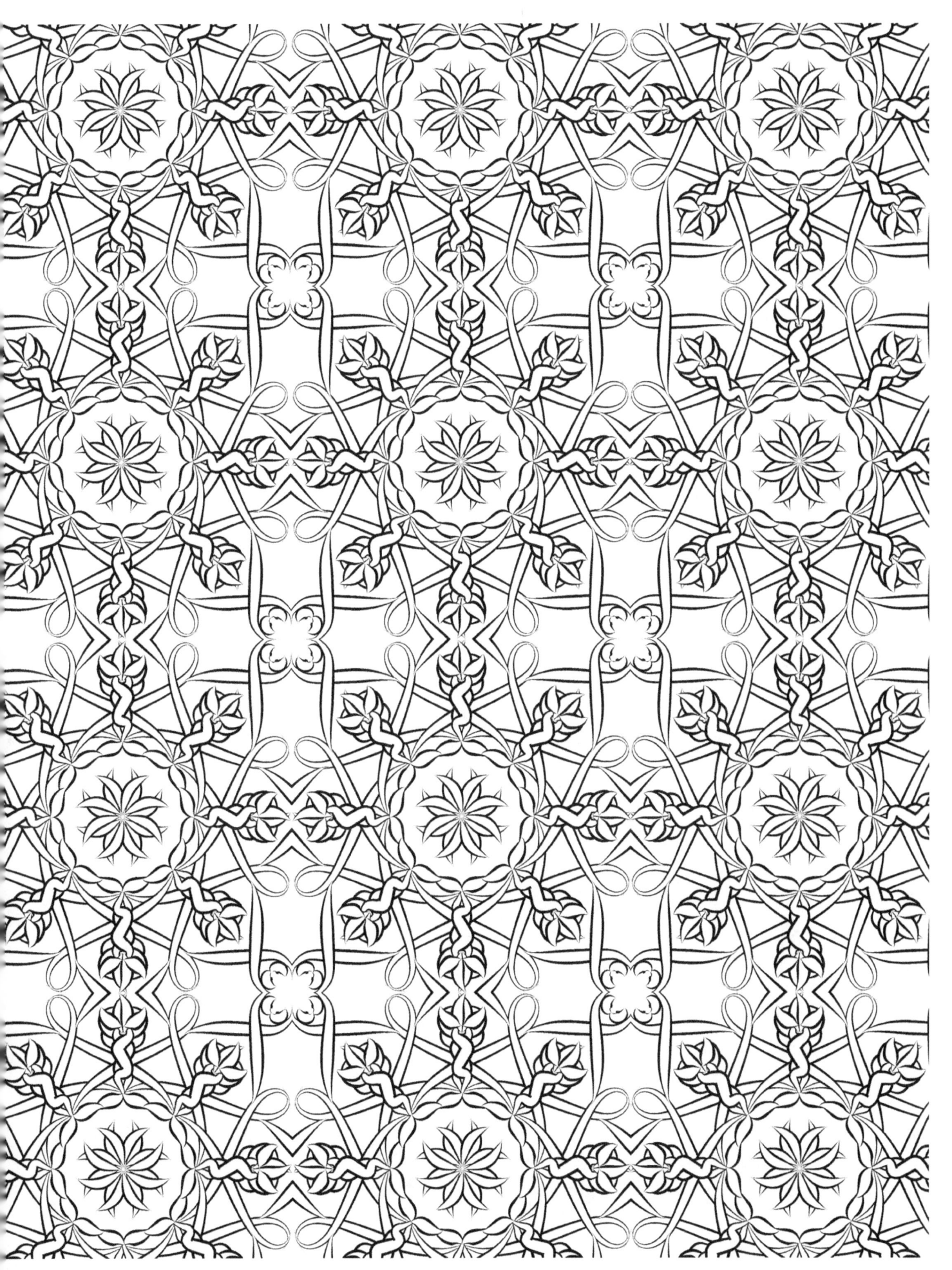

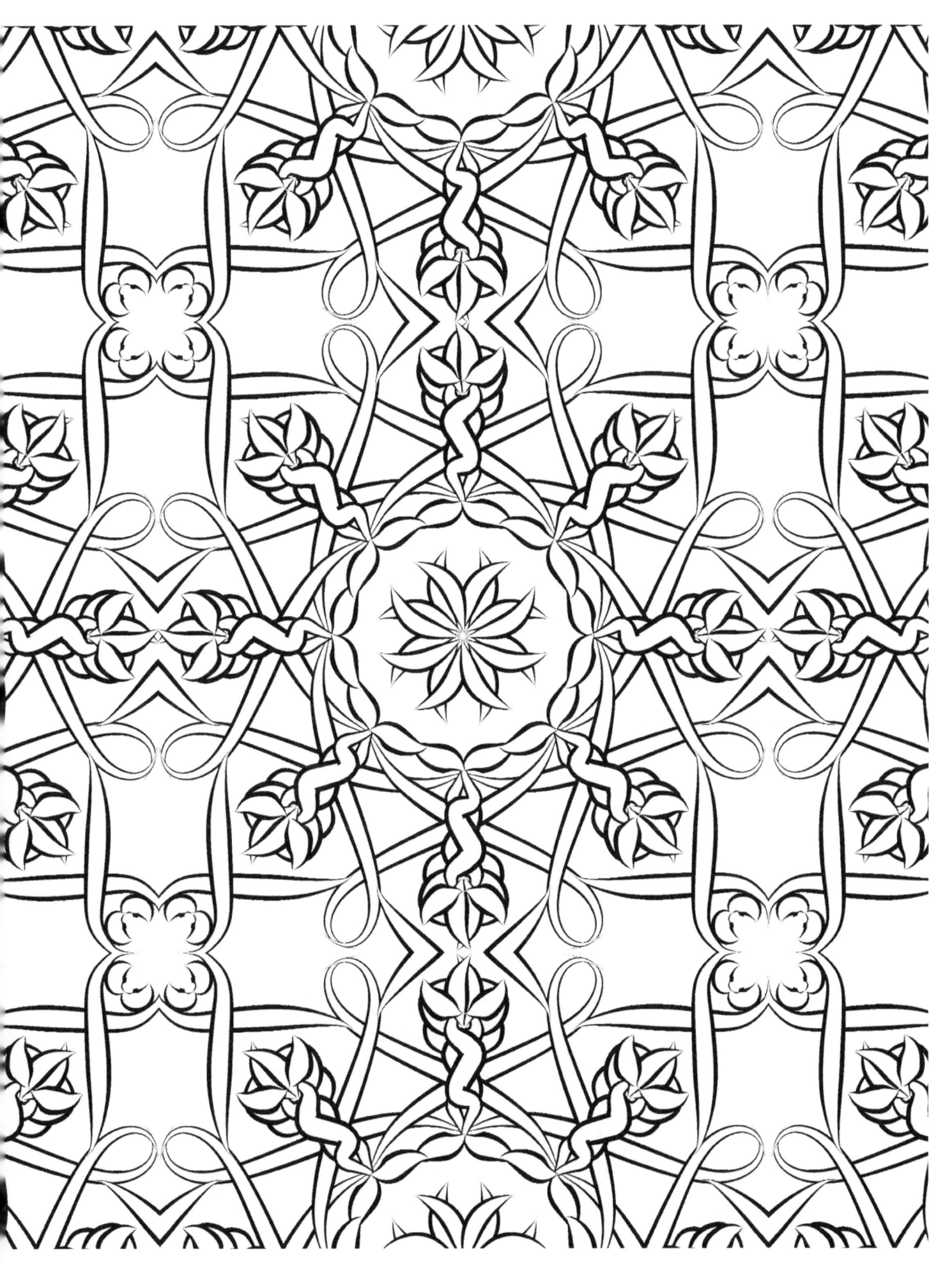

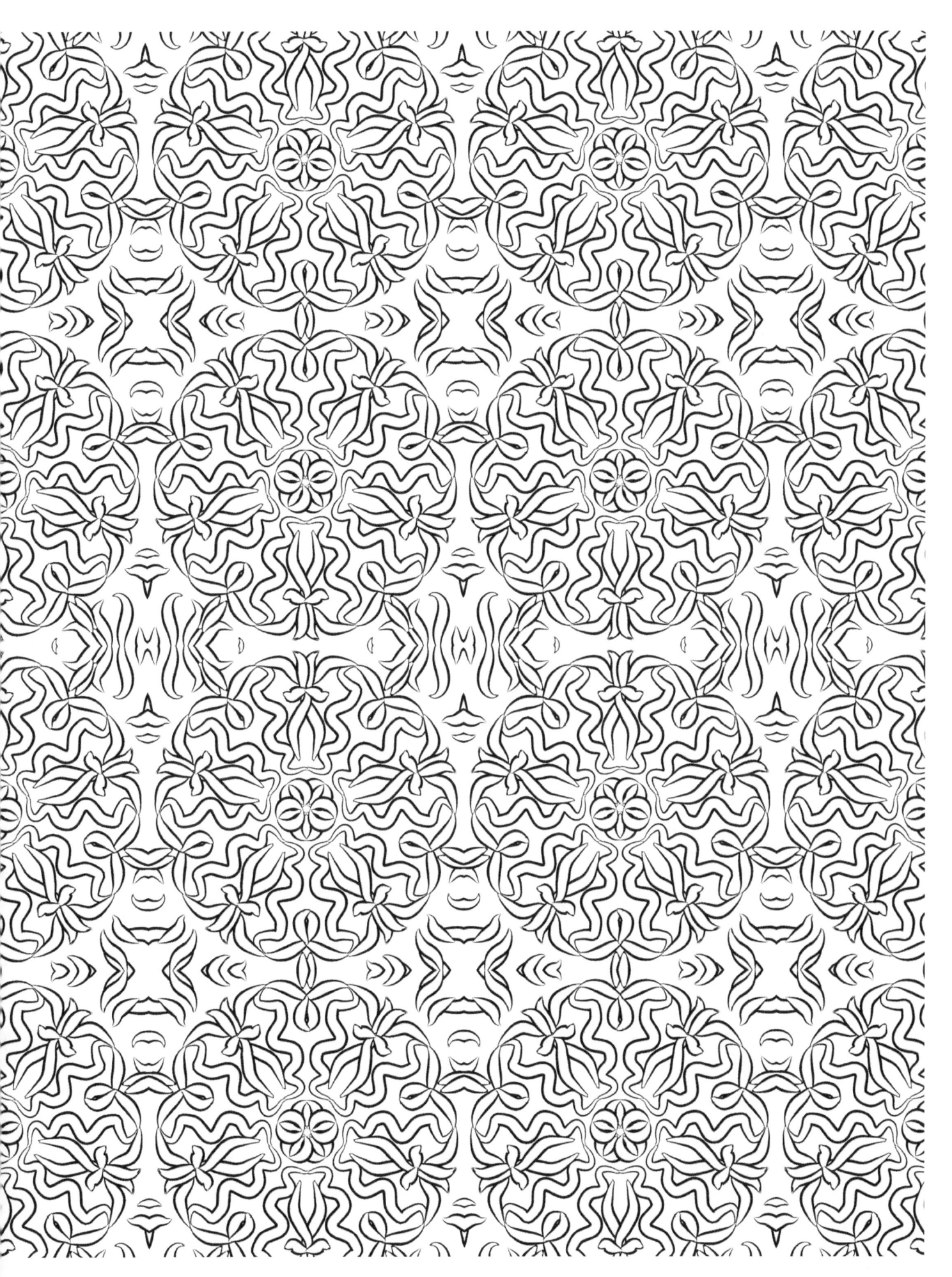

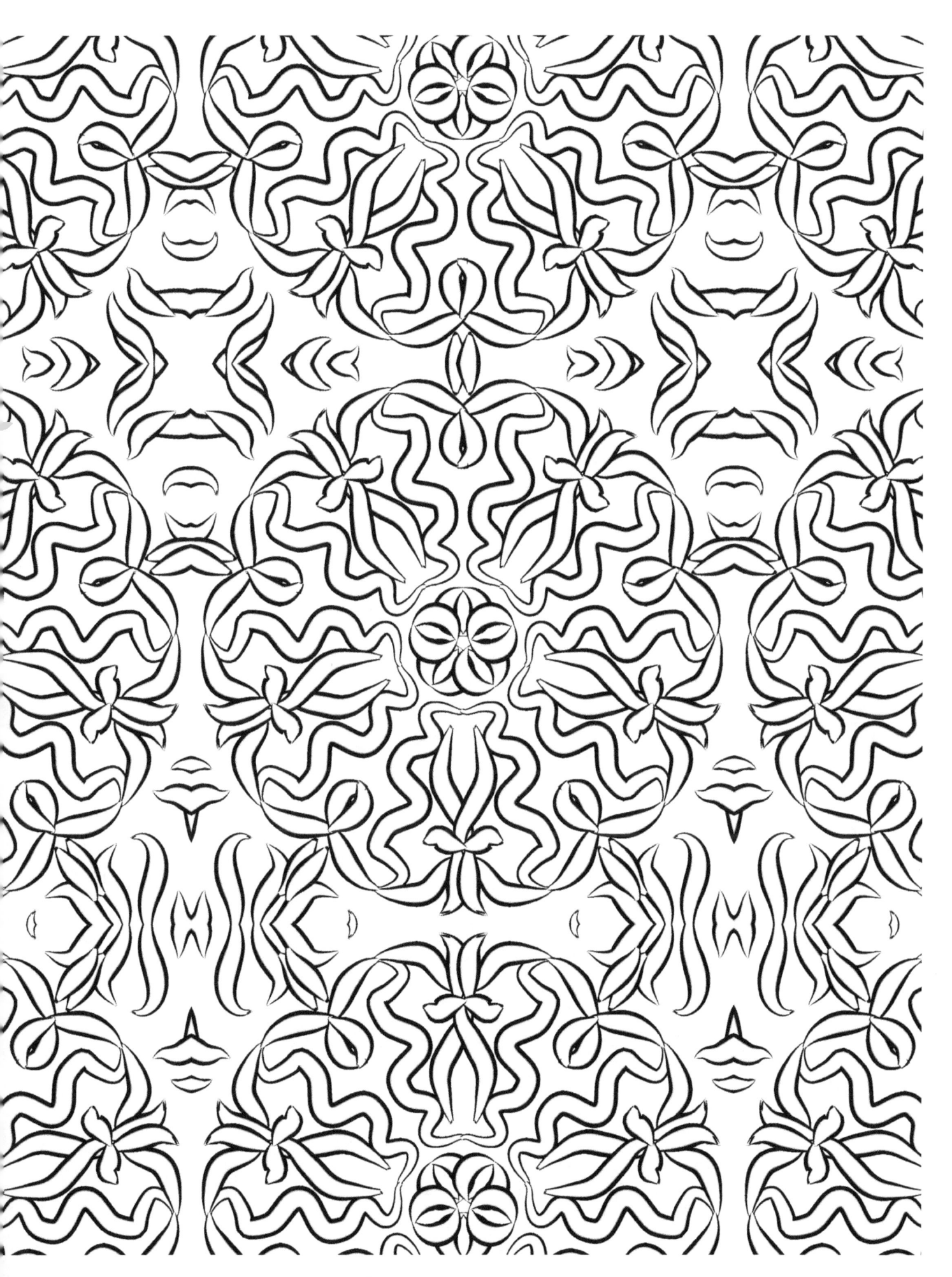

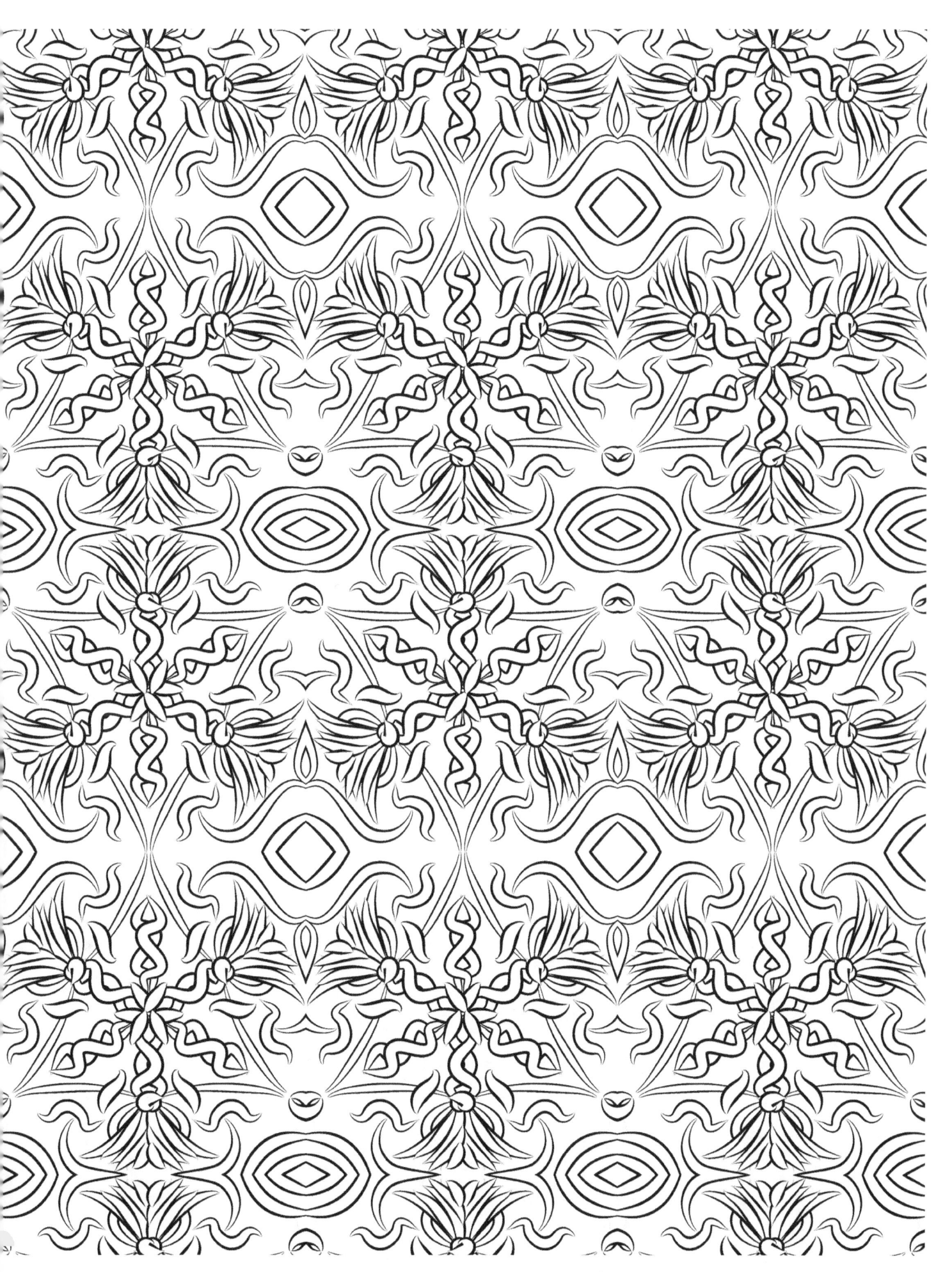

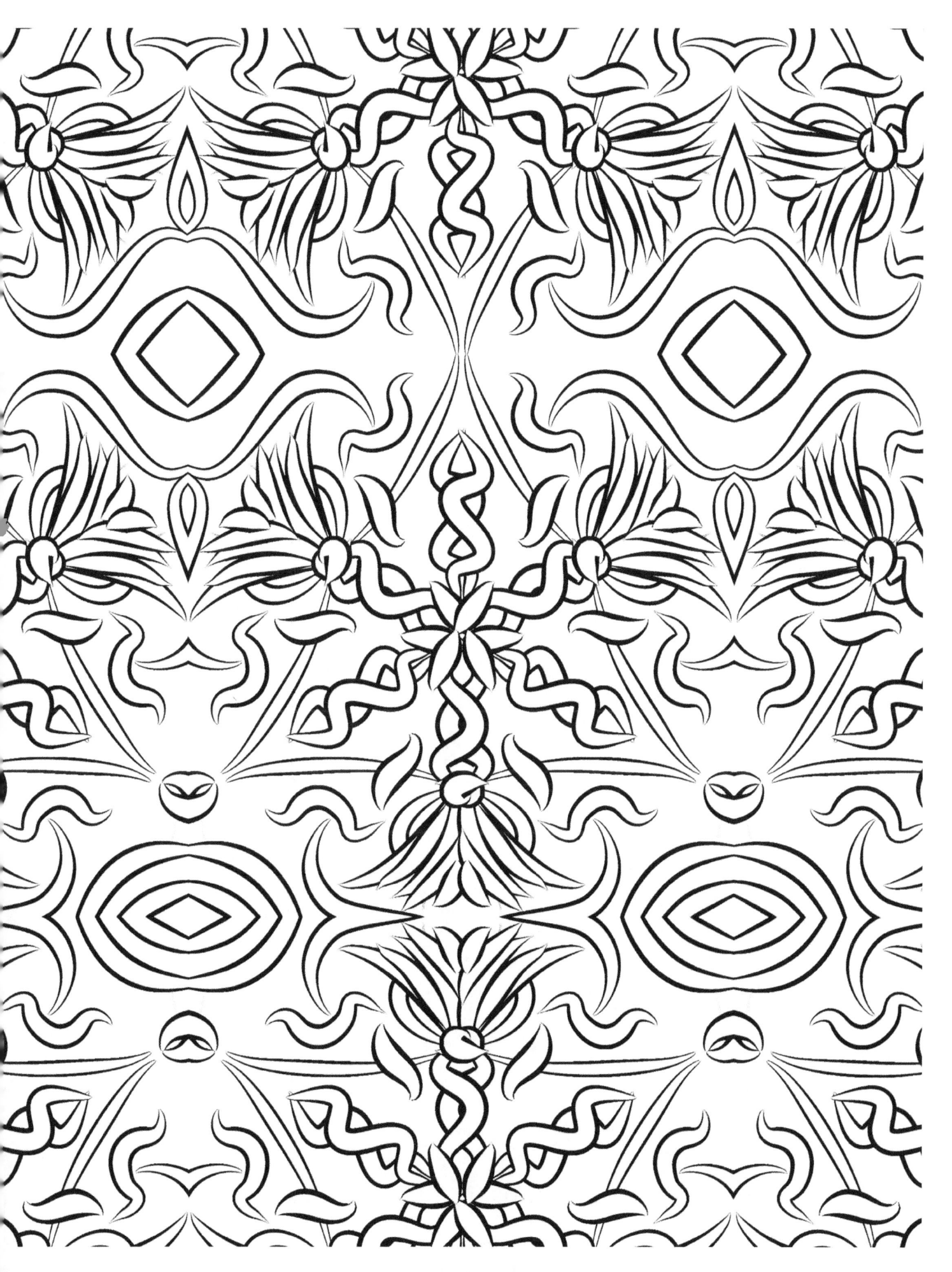

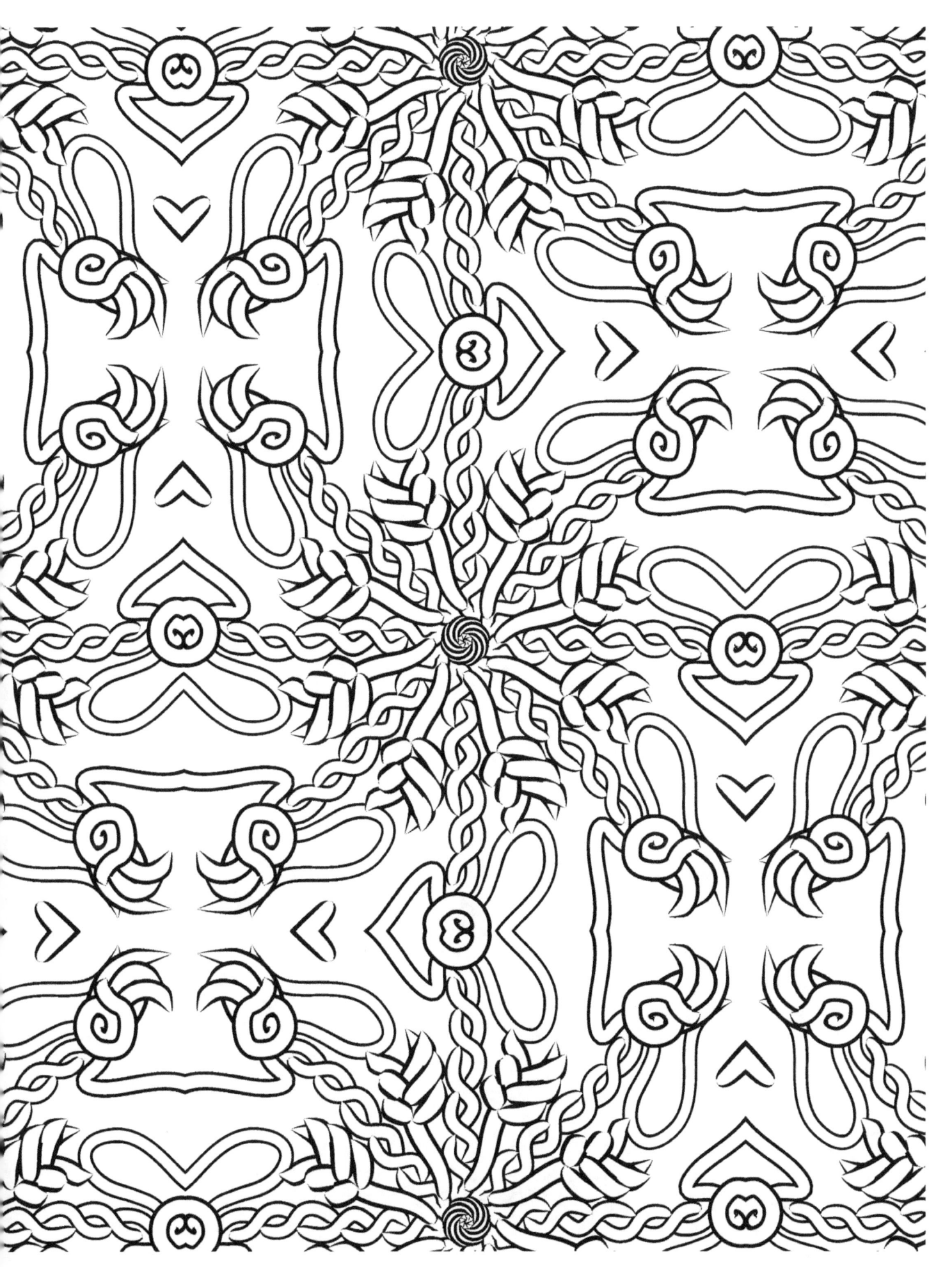

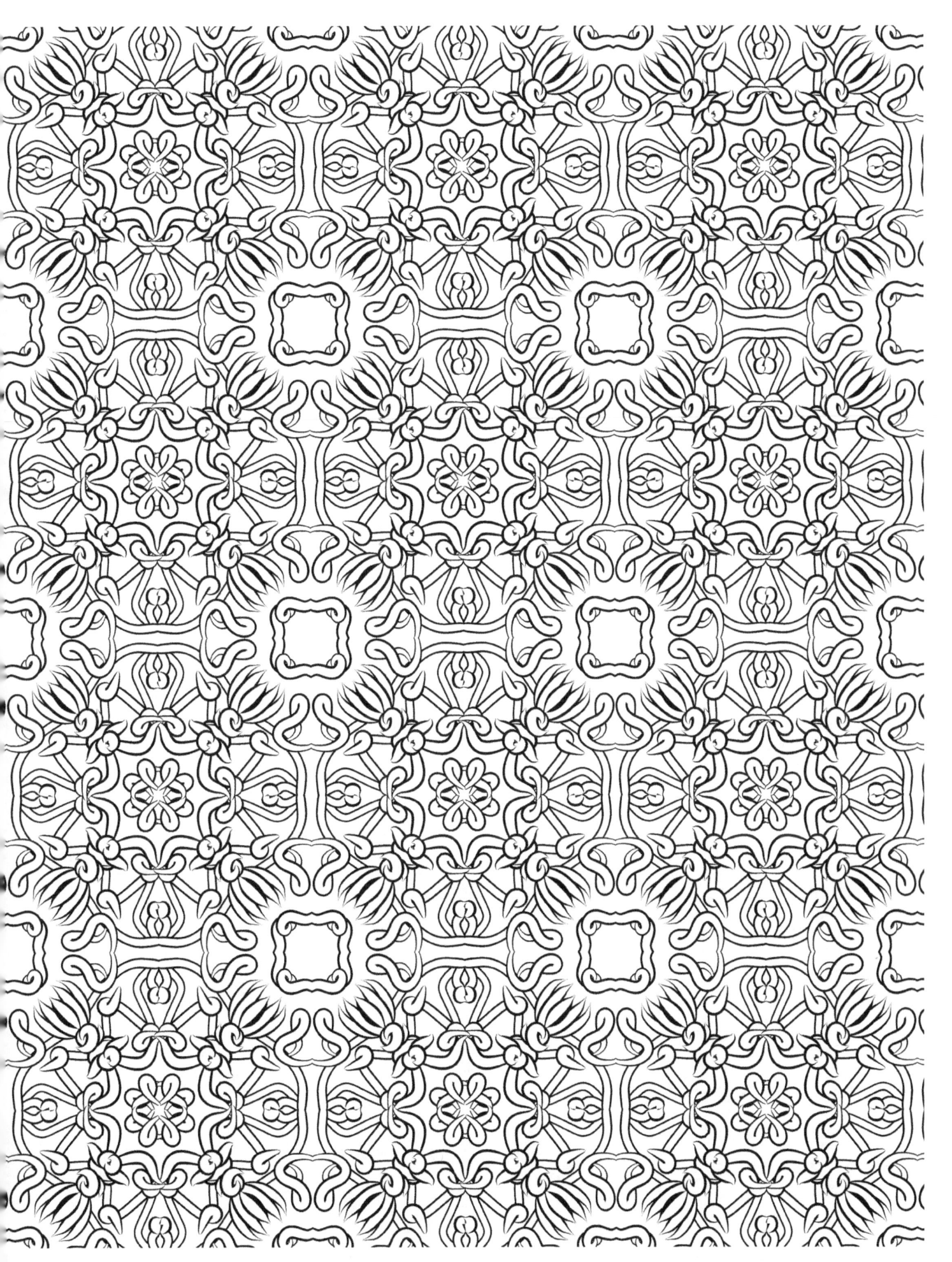

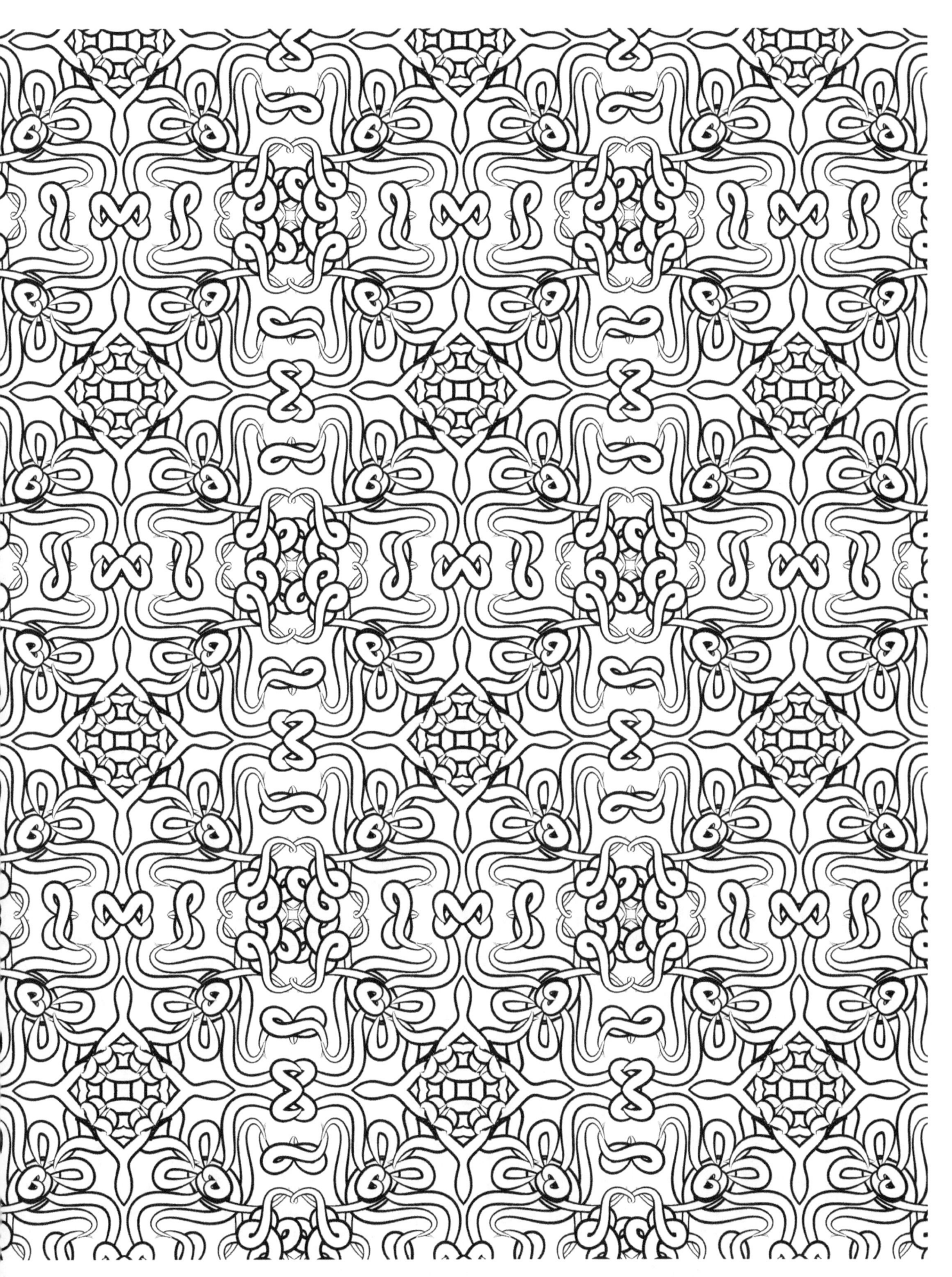

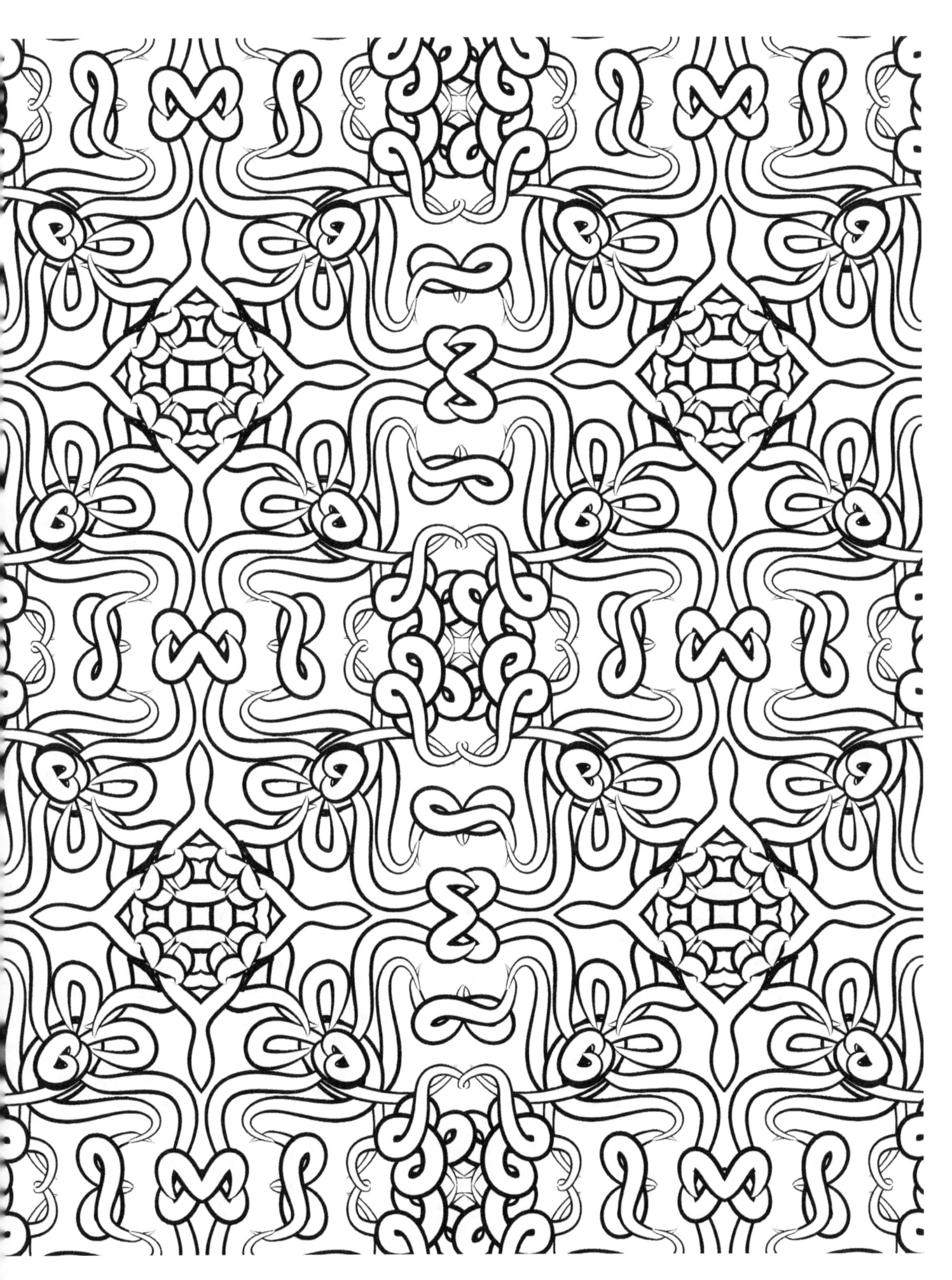

For more designs and upcoming books, please visit our
facebook group at :

@coloringbooksandmandalas